Hauptschule
BAYERN

ENGLISH H

Highlight

1

Cornelsen

ENGLISH H
HIGHLIGHT
BAND 1

Im Auftrage des Verlages herausgegeben und erarbeitet von

Roderick Cox, Aachen ▪ Raymond Williams, York

Ausgabe für Bayern erarbeitet von
Raymond Williams sowie Roderick Cox

Verlagsredaktion

Frank Donoghue (Projektleitung),
Karin Jung (verantwortliche Redakteurin),
Murdo MacPhail, Grit Ellen Sellin, Rolf Wiesemes
und Birgit Herrmann, Aachen (Außenredaktion)

Beratende Mitwirkung

Bill Dugent, Zusmarshausen ▪ Gerhard Eichner,
Nürnberg ▪ Kunigunde Fraas, Würzburg
Gottfried Furtner, Unterammergau ▪ Angelika Hillen,
München ▪ Eveline Jakob-Bertl, München
Gabi Krista, Lohr ▪ Rosemarie Meyerhoff, Lichtenau
Adele Rump, Dingolfing ▪ Rudolf Schlossbauer,
Erlangen ▪ Ludwig Waas, München ▪ Renate Winter,
Deggendorf ▪ Petra Würschinger, Regensburg

Grafik

Donald Gott, London
Kate Taylor, Bradford
Skip G. Langkafel, Berlin
Katharina Wieker, Berlin

Umschlaggestaltung

Knut Waisznor

Layout

Lynn Whittemore, Boston (USA)

Technische Umsetzung

Gisela Hoffmann

┌───┐
│ **Begleitende Tonträger zu diesem Band** │
│ Text-Cassette zum Schülerbuch (Best.-Nr. 78051) │
│ Text-CDs zum Schülerbuch (Best.-Nr. 77926) │
└───┘

 http://www.cornelsen.de

1. Auflage   €
Druck 8 7 6 5   Jahr 04 03 02 01

Alle Drucke dieser Auflage sind inhaltlich
unverändert und können im Unterricht nebeneinander
verwendet werden.

Druck: CS-Druck Cornelsen Stürtz, Berlin

ISBN 3-464-07788-8

Bestellnummer 77888

 Gedruckt auf säurefreiem Papier,
umweltschonend hergestellt aus chlorfrei gebleichten Faserstoffen.

INHALT

[ ] Rezeptiv   (Strukturen, die nur verstanden werden sollen)
＊ Fakultativ   (wahlfreie Bestandteile des Lehrwerks)

3

4

Start here ...

Germany is in Europe.
England is in Europe, too.

Chester is in England. Chester is a town in England.

SHARON I'm from Chester.
I'm from Elm Road.
Here's my house.
My house is number 6.

DAVE I'm from Elm Road, too.
Here's my house.
My house is number 5.

ASIF I'm from Chester, too.
I'm from London Road.
Here's my flat.
My flat is above a shop.

CLAIRE I'm from Elm Road.
Here's my house.
My house is number 10.
I'm new in Elm Road. W 1

* Die blau gedruckten Verweise bezeichnen den frühestmöglichen Einsatzort der Übungen im Workbook.
W 1 = Workbook, Übung 1 der jeweiligen Unit

I'm **7**

EXERCISE ■ **10 or 11?**

1

I'm Sharon Glenn.
I'm from Elm Road.
I'm at Brookland School.
And I'm 11.

2

I'm Dave Kelly.
… from Elm Road.
… at Brookland School.
And … 11.

3

… Asif Ahmed.
… London Road.
… Brookland School.
And … 10.

4

… Claire Hall.
… Elm Road.
… Brookland School.
… 10.

5

… Martin Feldmann.
… Weimarer Straße.
… Goldberg-Schule.
… 10.

And you?
I'm …
I'm from …
I'm at …
And I'm …

W 2-5

8

English numbers

1 one	**2** two	**3** three	**4** four	**5** five	**6** six
7 seven	**8** eight	**9** nine	**10** ten	**11** eleven	**12** twelve

SONG  Start again …

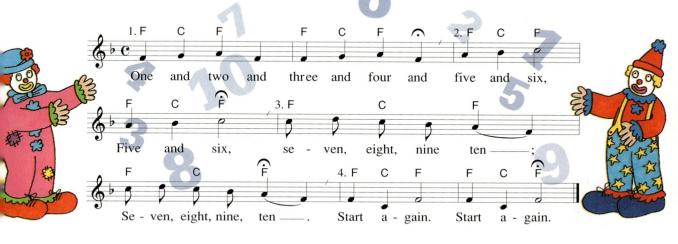

One and two and three and four and five and six,

Five and six, se - ven, eight, nine ten ———;

Se - ven, eight, nine, ten ———. Start a - gain. Start a - gain.

ACTIVITY A name card for your English lesson

I'm Sabine Bauer.
My English name
is Susan.

✔ CHECKPOINT

Was deine Lehrerin / dein Lehrer im Unterricht sagt:

Look here, please.

Write exercise 1, please.

Listen, please.

Open your books, please.

W 6-7

9

UNIT ONE
Hallo! 🎧

A Here's Elm Road. Elm Road is a road in Chester.

B

CLAIRE	Hallo. I'm new here. I'm Claire Hall. What's your name?
ASIF	My name is Asif Ahmed. Where are you from?
CLAIRE	I'm from Elm Road. My house is number 10.
ASIF	I'm from London Road. How old are you?
CLAIRE	I'm 10.

> **And you?**
> What's your name?   – I'm …
> Where are you from?   – I'm from …
> How old are you?   – I'm …

W 1

C

ASIF	Hallo, Dave.
DAVE	Hallo.
CLAIRE	I'm Claire. I'm new here.
DAVE	What's your badge?
	Are you a Manchester City fan?
CLAIRE	Yes, I am.
DAVE	Ugh! A City fan!
	Are you stupid?
CLAIRE	No, I'm not. You're stupid.
	And you're very unfriendly, too.
ASIF	Manchester City is a terrible football team.
	I'm a Manchester United fan.

D

CLAIRE	DAVE
What's your name?	Dave Kelly.
Are you from London Road?	No, I'm not.
	I'm from Elm Road.
And are you at Brookland School?	Yes, I am.
Oh, no!	

EXERCISE 1 ■ **Dave and Claire**

DAVE	CLAIRE
… name?	Claire Hall.
… London Road?	No, I'm not.
	I'm from Elm Road.
… at Brookland School?	Yes, I am.
… 10?	Yes, I am.

YOU	A PARTNER
Are you new here?	– Yes, I am.
Are you from Elm Road?	– No, I'm not.
Are you at Brookland School?	
Are you at … Schule?	
Are you 11?	
Are you a football fan?	
Are you from England?	
Are you in Germany?	

W 2

E Claire is a football fan.

Asif is a football fan.

Claire and Asif are fans.
They're football fans.
Manchester City and Manchester United are teams.
They're football teams. W 3

F

MRS HALL Are they from Elm Road?
CLAIRE Dave is from number 5.
Asif is a boy from London Road.

MRS HALL Are they nice?
CLAIRE No. They're unfriendly.
And they're at my new school, too.
MRS HALL But Brookland School is a big school.
Perhaps they're in a different class.

EXERCISE 2 ■ They're …

They're from Chester. ▪ They're 10.
They're at Brookland School. ▪ They're football fans.
They're from Elm Road. ▪ They're boys.
They're new in Elm Road.

1 Dave and Asif
They're from Chester.
They're at Brookland School.
They're boys.

2 Dave and Claire
They're from Chester.
They're at Brookland School.
They're from …

3 Claire and Asif
They're …
They're …
They're …
They're …

4 Claire and Mrs Hall

5 Dave, Asif, Claire and Mrs Hall

1

G

H Brookland School is in Chester. It's a big school.
Claire is at Brookland School. She's in Class 6A.
Dave is at Brookland School. He's in Class 6A, too.

EXERCISE 3 ■ Class 6A and Class 6B

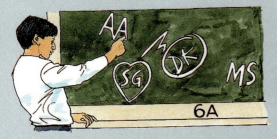 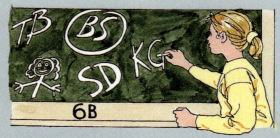

1 Asif Ahmed is at Brookland School.
  He's in Class 6A.
2 Kate Green is at Brookland School.
  She's in Class …

3 Mike Steel is …
  He's in …
4 Tina Baker …
  She's in …

5 Sharon Glenn …
6 Sarah Dean …
7 Ben Smith …
8 Dave Kelly …

EXERCISE 4 ■ Quiz: He's/She's/It's …

1 He's "MS" in Class 6A.
  – *He's Mike Steel.*
2 She's a teacher. – *She's …*

3 It's a school. It's in Chester.
4 He's in Class 6A. He's 11.
5 She's a football fan. She's at school with Dave.

W 4

I

CLAIRE I'm at Brookland School.

DAVE AND ASIF We're at Brookland School, too.

W 5

STORY 🎧

Claire is at a new school. She's in Class 6A, with Dave Kelly.

New friends?

CLAIRE Oh, you! Dave Kelly!
Are you in Class 6A, too?
DAVE Yes, I am.
SHARON Hi, Claire. I'm Sharon.
5 Are you and Dave friends?
CLAIRE Friends? No. He's terrible.
SHARON Dave is OK – for a boy.
MRS BROWN OK! It's maths now.
Open your maths books, please.
10 Exercise 4 and exercise 5.

DAVE Ugh, maths. It's terrible.
CLAIRE Maths is OK.
DAVE OK? And exercise 4?
CLAIRE I'm at exercise 5.
Exercise 4 is OK. Here ... 15
DAVE Thank you, Claire.
You're good at maths.

MIKE	Dave Kelly is with a girl!
PETE	Hallo, Dave.
MIKE	Hallo – Mrs Kelly.
PETE	Are you a new girlfriend?
CLAIRE	No, I'm not. You boys are stupid.
DAVE	Yes. You're very unfriendly.
	Claire is new here.
CLAIRE	Thank you, Dave. You're right.
	They're very unfriendly.
DAVE	But we're friends now. I'm sorry, Claire.
	You're OK – for a Manchester City fan.

20 (line marker)
25 (line marker)

TASK A ■ Right or wrong?

1 Dave and Claire are in Class 6B.
2 Dave is in a different class.
3 Sharon is with Claire and Dave.
4 Maths is terrible for Dave.
5 Exercise 4 is a maths exercise.
6 Dave is with a girlfriend.
7 Mike and Pete are unfriendly.
8 Claire and Dave are friends now.

TASK B ■ Wie beantwortet Claire Petes Fragen?

Yes, I am. ▪ No, I'm not.

1 Are you new at Brookland School?
2 Are you in Class 6B?
3 Are you from Elm Road?
4 Are you a football fan?
5 Are you a Manchester United fan?
6 Are you a Manchester City fan?

W 6-8

ACTIVE ENGLISH

ACTIONS 🎧 Begrüßung und Verabschiedung

Wie begrüßen sich diese Personen? Wie verabschieden sie sich?
Schreibe zwei Listen.

Hallo, Pat. – Hi.

Hallo, Mum. – Hallo, Tim.

Good afternoon, Mr Green.
– Good afternoon, Emma.

See you. – Bye.

Goodbye. – Bye-bye.

Good morning, Mrs Hill.
– Good morning, Martin.

Good evening.
– Hallo, Alan.

EXERCISE 1 ■ Suche dir Personen aus. Wie begrüßen sie sich?

EXERCISE 2 ■ Wie verabschieden sie sich?

Sally Steel

Mrs Steel

Peter

Alan

Mr Ambrose

Mrs Khan

W 9-10

ACTIVITY My English badge

LOOK AROUND YOU English words in Germany

In Deutschland kannst du oft englische Wörter hören oder lesen.

- Dir fallen bestimmt einige ein. Schreibe sie auf.
- Suche in alten Zeitschriften oder Katalogen nach weiteren Wörtern.
- Gestaltet damit gemeinsam ein Poster für euer Klassenzimmer.

W 11

PRACTICE PAGES

STRUCTURES

EXERCISE 1 ■ **Jörg schreibt seinem Brieffreund. Was schreibt er: am ▪ is ▪ are?**

I … 11. I … from Germany. Tanja and Petra are in my photo, too. They … 9. We … from Bavaria. My school … in Würzburg. It … a big town. My teacher is OK. He … nice. Tanja and Petra … at a different school. It … new. You … from Chester. … it a big town?

✔ **CHECKPOINT**

Langformen
am   I am
is   he is, she is, it is
are you are, we are, they are

EXERCISE 2 ■ **English badges: Welche Sprüche stehen darauf?**

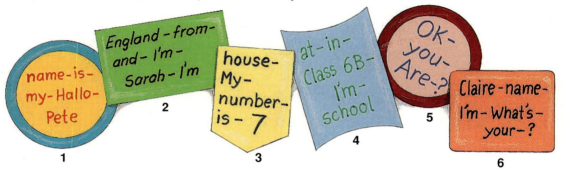

EXERCISE 3 ■ **Kannst du die Kurzformen vervollständigen?**

CLAIRE Here's a nice photo. I… in my house.
Here's my new house. It… OK.
And here's my mum. She… in Elm Road.
Here's Tom. He… 8.
Oh, yes. Mum and I. We… in Chester.
Here are my friends. They… in London.
And Dave, you… in a photo, too.
Here's Asif. He… with a friend.

✔ **CHECKPOINT**

Kurzformen
'm   I'm
's   he's, she's, it's
're you're, we're, they're

W 12-16

18

SITUATIONS

Wie fragst du auf Englisch, …

1 … wie jemand heißt? (Are you new here? / What's your name?)

2 … wo jemand herkommt? (I'm from Chester. / Where are you from?)

3 … ob jemand hier neu ist? (Are you new here? / Is it new here?)

4 … ob jemand aus England kommt? (Are you in England? / Are you from England?)

Tipp: Die richtigen Fragen findest du auf den Seiten 10-16.

WORDPOWER

WORDPOWER 1 ■ He, she, it?

1	Asif - *he*	9	house
2	Claire	10	Tom
3	road	11	shop
4	girlfriend	12	boy
5	England	13	teacher
6	Mrs Hall	14	Europe
7	school	15	Mrs Brown
8	Mr Ahmed	16	badge

WORDPOWER 2 ■ Paare

• Germany	• she
• house	• See you.
• yes	• England
• girl	• flat
• morning	• no
• he	• afternoon
• Goodbye.	• boy

WORDPOWER 3 ■ Wer hat den Geheimzettel geschrieben? Es fehlen die Buchstaben a, e, i, o, u.

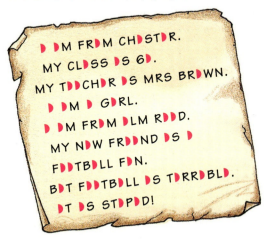

WORDPOWER 4 ■ Kannst du die Briefe in die richtigen Säcke werfen?

W 17-19

SOUNDS

[d]: Dave, England, road, and, old, friend, good

[t]: teacher, town, terrible, at, it, not, flat

SPECIAL TOPIC

In your classroom

1   Pupils in English lessons

EXERCISE 1 ■ **Can we have a …, please?**

1   story   2   song

3   game   4   video

EXERCISE 2 ■ **What's … in English?**

1   *freundlich*   2   *Tisch*

3   *Hund*   4   *nett*

EXERCISE 3 ■ **What's … in German?**

1   *pencil*   2   *town*

3   *dog*   4   *train*

W 20

2   Teachers in English lessons

EXERCISE 4 ■ **Was sagt die Lehrerin?**

- Listen, please.
- Look here, please.
- Open your books, please.
- Write exercise 3, please.

1   2

3   4

3 In a pencil-case

a pen
b rubber
c ruler
d felt-tip
e biro
f pencil

> **What's in your pencil-case?**
> A pen,
> two pencils, …
>
> W 21

SONG 🎧 Pen and pencil

Pen and pencil, ruler, book, ruler, book,
Pen and pencil, ruler, book, ruler, book,
And felt-tip, biro, bag and board,
Pen and pencil, ruler, book, ruler, book.

LISTENING 🎧 At school

Welche Klasse macht was?

Number 1 is in Class …   Number 3 is in Class …   Number 5 is in Class …
Number 2 is in Class …   Number 4 is in Class …   Number 6 is in Class …

Class 7B

Class 6C

Class 7A

Class 7C

Class 6B

Class 6A

W 22-23

SUMMARY

am – is – are

I'm from Hill Road.

Sam is 11.

Tim and Pat are at school.

I'm a teacher. Ich bin Lehrer/Lehrerin.
We're friends. Wir sind Freunde/Freundinnen.
Tina is my new friend. Tina ist meine neue Freundin.
Pat and Adam are from Chester. Pat und Adam sind aus Chester.

AUSSAGEN

I am	
You are	
He is	
She is	in my house.
It is	
We are	
You are	
They are	

Das sind die Langformen.

Und das sind die Kurzformen.

I'm	
You're	
He's	
She's	in my house.
It's	
We're	
You're	
They're	

Kurzformen sind sehr häufig. Sie werden gesprochen und oft auch geschrieben.
Wenn du sie schreibst, zeigt das Auslassungszeichen ('), dass ein oder mehrere
Buchstaben weggefallen sind.

FRAGEN UND KURZANTWORTEN

Are you	from Germany?	– Yes, I am.
	at Brookland School?	– No, I'm not.
	from Chester?	
	11?	

	MRS HILL	**SALLY**
Hallo. Are you from number 4?		Yes, I am.
		I'm new here.
Are you at Brookland School?		Yes, I am.
Are you in Class 6B?		No, I'm not.
		I'm in Class 6A.

IN DIESER UNIT HAST DU GELERNT, ...

... Auskunft über dich zu geben. ➠ *My name is Claudia. I'm 10.*
I'm from Germany.

... Auskunft über andere einzuholen. ➠ *What's your name?*
How old are you?
Where are you from?

... jemanden zu begrüßen. ➠ *Hallo./Hi.*
Good morning/afternoon/evening.

... dich zu verabschieden. ➠ *Goodbye. / Bye-bye. / See you.*

... dich für etwas zu entschuldigen. ➠ *I'm sorry.*

... im Unterricht um etwas zu bitten. ➠ *Can we have a song, please?*

... nach einem englischen Wort zu fragen. ➠ *What's* Auto *in English?*

DU KANNST AUCH VERSTEHEN, WIE ...

... eure Lehrerin / euer Lehrer euch ➠ *Listen, please.*
darum bittet, etwas zu tun. *Write exercise 1, please.*

UNIT TWO
At home 🎧

A

Here's a house.
It's English.
It's in a town.
It's a house with a garage
and a garden.

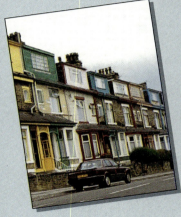

Here are some old houses.

Here are some new houses.

And here are some flats.

B

Here's a house in a village.
It's an English house.
It's an old house.

And your flat/house?	
It's	in a town.
	in a village.
	an old flat/house.
	a new flat/house.

C

Claire's family

Here's Claire Hall and her family.
They're in front of 10 Elm Road.

Sharon's family

They're in front of number 6.
Sharon Glenn is next to her mother.
Terry is Sharon's dog.

Dave's family

"I'm Dave Kelly. I'm from 5 Elm Road.
I'm in my garden. I'm with my parents,
my brother and my cat, Boris. He's very
big. Boris and Terry are neighbours.
But they aren't friends!"

Asif Ahmed's family

They aren't from Elm Road.
They're from London Road.
Asif is next to his big sisters.
Grandma Ahmed is from Pakistan.

W 1

EXERCISE 1 ■ Four families

Claire's family
Sharon's family
Dave's family
Asif's family

They're They aren't	from London Road. from Elm Road. a big family. in front of a house. in front of a shop. in a garden.

W 2

D Asif is at home. He's in the flat.
The flat is big, with four bedrooms and four other rooms.
The kitchen is next to the living-room.
The toilet is next to the bathroom.
Asif's bedroom is small.

And your flat/house?
It's big/small, with … rooms.
My bedroom / The kitchen /… is …

E

Asif is in the flat. He's in his bedroom.

Aysha isn't in her bedroom.
She's in the living-room.

Asif's grandma is in the kitchen.

Bina isn't in the kitchen.
She's in the bathroom.

EXERCISE 2 ■ **He/She isn't …**

1 Asif is in his bedroom. He isn't in the kitchen. He isn't in the bathroom. He isn't in …
2 Aysha is in the … She isn't in … She isn't in …
3 Asif's grandma is in the … She isn't in …
4 Bina is in the … She isn't in …

W 3

F And where are Mr and Mrs Ahmed?
They're in the shop.
It's open from 8 in the morning till 10 in the evening.
The name? – *8 till late*.

G

DAVE	You're lucky! Your flat is above a shop. It's a good shop. Is it a busy shop?
ASIF	Yes, it is.
DAVE	Is a family shop fun?
ASIF	No, it isn't. Is your mum at home in the evenings?
DAVE	Yes, she is.
ASIF	Is your dad busy in the evenings?
DAVE	No, he isn't.
ASIF	Well, my parents are busy till very late.
DAVE	But the things in your shop are good. – And videos are free for you!

EXERCISE 3 ■ Dave is at home with his mum.

1 **MRS KELLY**   Is the shop open till late?
  DAVE   Yes, it is. / No, it isn't.
2 Is Asif's mum at home in the evenings?
  Yes, she is. / No, she isn't.
3 Is she in the shop in the evenings?
  Yes, she is. / No, she isn't.
4 Is Asif's dad at home in the evenings?
  Yes, he is. / No, he isn't.
5 Is he in the shop till late?
  Yes, he is. / No, he isn't.
6 Is the shop very busy?
  Yes, it is. / No, it isn't.

YOU
Is your mum/dad busy in the evenings?
Is your flat/house big/small/OK?

A PARTNER
– Yes,	he is.	– No,	he isn't.
	she is.		she isn't.
	it is.		it isn't.

W 4

H   Dave and Asif are in the shop.

Look, Asif. Here's a new *Superdog* video.

OK. It's a free video for you. Let's go.

I'm a good customer here.

Yes – for free videos!

STORY 🎧

A family shop isn't always fun.

Lucky Asif?

Sharon is in Mr and Mrs Ahmed's shop.

SHARON	Video number 99, please.
MRS AHMED	Video 99? … I'm sorry, but the video isn't here. What is it?
5 **SHARON**	*Superdog.*
MRS AHMED	No, it isn't in the shop. And it isn't in our flat. Our video recorder is broken.
SHARON	Oh. And the TV programmes
10	aren't very good today.
MRS AHMED	It's a nice evening. TV isn't everything.
SHARON	Well, never mind. Goodbye, Mrs Ahmed.

ASIF	Hallo, Mum.	15
MRS AHMED	Hallo, Dave. Hallo, Asif. The *Superdog* video isn't here, Asif.	
ASIF	Er, *Superdog?*	
MRS AHMED	And it isn't in our video recorder.	20
	Our video recorder is broken.	
DAVE	The video recorder at *our* house is OK.	
MRS AHMED	What? Is the video at your house?	
ASIF	Er, not now.	25
DAVE	No, here's the video.	

MR AHMED	Aha – here's the video. But our customer isn't here now.
DAVE	What customer?
MRS AHMED	Sharon Glenn.
DAVE	It's OK. Her house is in Elm Road. She's my neighbour.
	It's only five minutes from here.
ASIF	Let's go, Dave.
MRS AHMED	Just a minute. Two pounds for the video, please. It isn't free.
MR AHMED	No, our videos aren't free. But *Superdog* is free for Sharon now.
	£1 from Asif and £1 from Dave, please.
DAVE	Perhaps a family shop isn't always fun.
ASIF	And videos aren't always good.
DAVE	No, *Superdog* is terrible!

(line numbers: 30, 35)

TASK A ■ **Yes, it is. / No, it isn't.**

1 Is video number 99 in the shop?
2 Is it in the flat?
3 Is the video recorder in Asif's
   flat broken?
4 Is Dave's video recorder OK?
5 Is the video at Dave's house now?
6 Is the video free for Sharon?

TASK B ■ **What are the right words?**

broken ▪ customer ▪ free ▪ fun
neighbour ▪ number ▪ shop ▪ video

1 *Superdog* is a …
2 It's … 99.
3 The video recorder is …
4 Sharon is a … for *Superdog*.
5 Sharon is Dave's …
6 Elm Road is five minutes from the …
7 *Superdog* is … for Sharon.
8 A family shop isn't always …

W 5-6

ACTIVE ENGLISH

ACTIONS 🎧 Fragen, wo etwas ist

Was hat Ann wohl vor?

ANN Where's the phone book, Mum?

MRS FOX It's in the kitchen.

Und was will Mr Fry?

MR FRY I'm from *Fry's TV Service*.
Is the TV in the living-room?

MR TATE Yes, it is.

EXERCISE ■ **A quiz with a partner**

a Where's the …?

YOU Where's the …?

A PARTNER It's in the bedroom/…

b Is the …?

YOU Is the … in the bedroom/…?

A PARTNER Yes, it is. / No, it isn't.

badge ▪ book ▪ cat ▪ computer ▪ dog ▪ pen
phone ▪ photo ▪ TV ▪ video ▪ video recorder

bedroom   **living-room**

W 7-8

30

ACTIVITY Our flat/house

Our flat
Here's our flat. It's in Kleiststraße.
It's a flat with a balcony.
My bedroom is OK, but it's small.
It's next to the bathroom.

Jens Töpfer

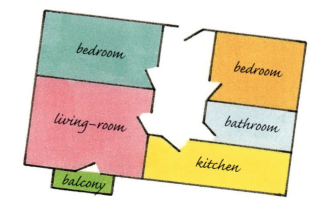

And your flat/house?

Here's our flat/house. It's in … Straße.
It's / It isn't a flat/house with a balcony/garden.

My bedroom is OK/nice/terrible/big/…
It's next to …
Our flat/house is OK / very nice /…

LOOK AROUND YOU TV programmes

In deutschen Fernsehzeitschriften findest du oft englische Bezeichnungen.
Welche gehört hier zu welcher Sendung?

Actionfilm ▪ Quiz ▪ Sciencefiction ▪ Talkshow ▪ Thriller ▪ Western

1

2

3

4

5

6

PRACTICE PAGES

STRUCTURES

EXERCISE 1 ■ Family quiz

1 Is Boris Dave's cat? – *Yes, he is.*
2 Is Sharon from 10 Elm Road? – *No, …*
3 Is Sharon Terry's sister?
4 Is Dave from 5 Elm Road?
5 Is Grandma Ahmed from Pakistan?
6 Is Asif from London Road?
7 Is Asif's bedroom big?
8 Is *8 till late* a shop?

EXERCISE 2 ■ Where are they?

1 They're at school. They *aren't* at home.
2 I'm in the house. I'*m not* in the garden.
3 We're in a shop. We … at school.
4 Asif is at Dave's house. He … at home.
5 She's in the garden. She … in the house.
6 You're at home. You … at school!
7 The videos are here. They … in the shop.
8 Our flat is in Chester. It … in London.

EXERCISE 3 ■ Lies zuerst die Antworten und suche dann die passenden Fragen.

- Are your parents always busy?
- Is your mum in the shop?
- Are we in London Road?
- Are you from here?
- Are you a customer?
- What's your name?
- Is *8 till late* a good shop?

1 …? – Yes, I am. I'm from London Road.
2 …? – Yes, we are.
3 …? – Yes, it is.
4 …? – No, I'm not! It's our shop.
5 …? – Yes, she is.
6 …? – Yes, they are.
7 …? – I'm …

– Wer hat die Fragen beantwortet?

EXERCISE 4 ■ Claire's, Asif's, Dave's, …

1 Claire's football is new.   2 …'s bedroom is small.   3 …'s cat is big.

4 … dog isn't very big.   5 … TV is broken.   6 … class is Class 6A.

W 10-11

SITUATIONS

Wie sagst du auf Englisch, dass …

1 … jemand Glück hat? (You're lucky. / You're good.)
2 … dir etwas Leid tut? (I'm busy. / I'm sorry.)
3 … etwas kaputt ist? (It's open. / It's broken.)
4 … etwas nicht kostenlos ist? (It isn't free. / It's for you.)

Tipp: Alle Sätze findest du auf den Seiten 24-30.

WORDPOWER

WORDPOWER 1 ■ Word families

> bathroom · brother · flat · grandma
> living-room · phone · school · shop
> sister · toilet · TV · video

1 mum, dad, …, …, …
2 video recorder, …, …, …
3 bedroom, kitchen, …, …, …
4 house, …, …, …

WORDPOWER 2 ■ What are they?

Tipp: Alle Wörter stehen in der Mehrzahl und enden auf -s.

1 stisser
2 sohsp
3 stonw
4 siveod
5 slaft
6 smoordeb 8 sobok   10 snapert
7 sargend   9 sindref   11 shoesu

WORDPOWER 3 ■ Small words

> above · at · for · from · in · till

1 Our flat is … a shop.
2 The shop is open … late.
3 Sharon and Luke are … school.
4 England is … Europe.
5 "Weißwürste" are … Bavaria.
6 The video is … my parents.

WORDPOWER 4 ■ a/an

1 Mr Tibbs is … very friendly teacher.
2 … evening in the shop isn't fun.
3 Terry is … small dog.
4 It's … nice evening.
5 Here's … old house.
6 Pat is … unfriendly girl. W 12-13

✔ CHECKPOINT

Vor Wörtern, die mit einem Vokallaut beginnen, verwendest du *an*, nicht *a*.
Here's **an** English book.
She's **an** old teacher.
He's **an** unfriendly boy.

SOUNDS 🎧

[s]: flats, parents, shops, toilets, books, cats
[z]: sisters, friends, families, rooms, videos
[ɪz]: classes, garages, exercises, houses [zɪz]

[ðə]: the book, the dog, the house, the pen
[ði]: the evening, the old dog, the exercise,
      the English book, the afternoon

SPECIAL TOPIC

Numbers

1	one	6	six
2	two	7	seven
3	three	8	eight
4	four	9	nine
5	five	10	ten

11	eleven
12	twelve
13	**thirteen**
14	fourteen
15	**fifteen**
16	sixteen
17	seventeen
18	eighteen
19	nineteen
20	twenty

21	twenty-one
22	twenty-two
...	
30	**thirty**
40	**forty**
50	**fifty**
60	sixty
70	seventy
80	eighty
90	ninety
100	a hundred

Write:
one = 1
seven = 7

EXERCISE ■ **Was sagt Pat?**

1 My house is number 23.
2 My friend Alan is at number ...
3 We're pop fans. We're Radio ... fans.
4 My bus is number ...
5 My friend is ... now.
6 Exercise ... is a maths exercise.
7 My mountain bike is number ...
8 I'm in Class ...

W 14-15

34

SONG 🎧 Ten green bottles

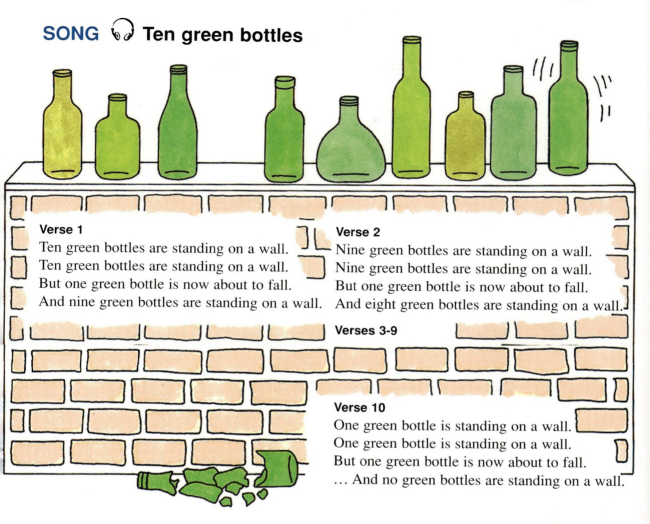

Verse 1

Ten green bottles are standing on a wall.
Ten green bottles are standing on a wall.
But one green bottle is now about to fall.
And nine green bottles are standing on a wall.

Verse 2

Nine green bottles are standing on a wall.
Nine green bottles are standing on a wall.
But one green bottle is now about to fall.
And eight green bottles are standing on a wall.

Verses 3-9

Verse 10

One green bottle is standing on a wall.
One green bottle is standing on a wall.
But one green bottle is now about to fall.
… And no green bottles are standing on a wall.

LISTENING 🎧 Videos from *8 till late*

What numbers are the five videos?

Sharon's video is number …
Mr Kelly's video is number …
Mrs Hall's video is number …

Mr Brown's video is number …
Mrs Steel's video is number …

W 16-17

SUMMARY

Genitive 's

Um zu zeigen, dass jemandem etwas gehört,
hängst du *'s* an den Namen oder das Nomen (*noun*) an.

It's Susan's shop.

Pat's T-shirt is new.
My **teacher's** house is old.
My **sister's** name is Bina.

am – is – are

VERNEINUNGEN

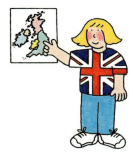

I'm from England.
I'm not from Germany.

The house is in a town.
It **isn't** in a village.

The boys are at school.
They **aren't** at home.

The video isn't in the shop. Das Video ist nicht im Laden.
The programmes aren't very good today. Die Sendungen sind heute nicht sehr gut.
Grandma Ahmed isn't in the kitchen. Oma Ahmed ist nicht in der Küche.

I'm not	
You aren't	
He isn't	
She isn't	from England.
It isn't	
We aren't	
You aren't	
They aren't	

Hier sind die Kurzformen.

I am not	
You are not	
He is not	
She is not	from England.
It is not	
We are not	
You are not	
They are not	

Hier sind die Langformen

2

FRAGEN UND KURZANTWORTEN

Is Nick from England? – Yes, he is.   Are they from Germany? – No, they aren't.

Is Julia 10? – Yes, she is. Ist Julia 10? – Ja.
Is Peter small? – No, he isn't. Ist Peter klein? – Nein.
Is the shop big? – Yes, it is. Ist der Laden groß? – Ja.
Are the videos good? – No, they aren't. Sind die Videos gut? – Nein.

Am I	
Are you	
Is he	
Is she	unfriendly?
Is it	
———	
Are we	
Are you	
Are they	

– Yes,	I am.
	you are.
	he is.
	she is.
	it is.
	———
	we are.
	you are.
	they are.

– No,	I'm not.
	you aren't.
	he isn't.
	she isn't.
	it isn't.
	———
	we aren't.
	you aren't.
	they aren't.

IN DIESER UNIT HAST DU GELERNT, ...

… zu sagen, wem etwas gehört.	⟹	It's Peter's dog.
… zu sagen, wie dir etwas gefällt.	⟹	It's OK/nice / very good / terrible.
… zu fragen, wo jemand oder etwas ist.	⟹	Where are the boys? Where's the book? Is it in the shop?
… zu sagen, wo jemand oder etwas ist.	⟹	He's in the kitchen. The video is next to the book.
… auf Englisch zu zählen.	⟹	one, two, three, …

UNIT THREE
At school 🎧

A The classroom in the photo is in England.
There's a teacher in the classroom.
There are some pupils in the classroom.

cupboard

window

door

teacher

board

pupil

bag

chair

table

EXERCISE 1 ■ **What's in the classroom?**

There's a teacher. There are some pupils.

There's a … There are some …

What's in your classroom?
There's a …
There are some …

W 1-3

B Mrs Brown is with her class at Brookland School.

MRS BROWN Listen, please. The class is in four groups for this lesson. Here are your jobs.

 Group 1:
Write exercise 3, please.

 Group 3:
Watch the film, please.

Group 2:
Read the story, please.

 Group 4:
Listen to the cassette, please.

EXERCISE 2 ■ Other jobs in lessons

1 … this video, please.
2 … the numbers in your books, please.
3 … the song, please.

Listen to ▪ Open ▪ Watch ▪ Write

4 … your maths books, please.

C Here are some other lessons with Class 6A.

Stand up, please.

Sit down, please.

Do this, please.

Put your hands up, please.

W 4

EXERCISE 3 ■ Game: Only do what O'Grady says …

O'Grady says, "Stand up, please."

Stand up, please.

Sorry, Pete.

D MRS BROWN

There's an open day at our school in ten days.
Money from the open day is for a new school minibus.
What are your ideas for the open day?

CLAIRE Let's have a parent-teacher football match.

PETE Let's bring sweets for a sweet stall.

SHARON Let's bring plants for a plant stall.

MARK Let's have a café.

Let's bring … ▪ Let's have …

EXERCISE 4 ■ Other ideas

1 … a tennis match.
2 … a video stall.
3 … CDs for a CD stall.

4 … cakes for a cake stall.
5 … a hockey match.
6 … comics for a comic stall.

W 5

E The open day is in five days. There are lots of jobs for the pupils. Class 6A is very busy.

Paint posters.
Write signs.
Make a video.
Plan stalls.

Sharon is painting a poster.
Pete is writing a sign.
Some girls are making a video.
Asif and Dave are planning a stall.

F

The school's open day is in two days.
Its open day is for a new minibus.
… open day is for pupils and parents.

This is Sharon's poster.
Her poster is very big.
… poster is in front of the school.

This is Pete's sign.
His sign is for a stall.
… sign is for the book stall.

Asif and Dave's idea is for a stall.
Their stall is a surprise.
… idea is very good.

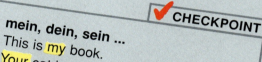

MRS BROWN
Here's my letter.
… letter is about the open day.

The letter is for your parents.
Please bring … parents to the open day.

There are lots of things at our open day.
… open days are fun.

✔ **CHECKPOINT**

mein, dein, sein …
This is **my** book.
Your cat is very big, Dave.
Pete Hill is in **his** room.
Mrs Hall is in **her** house.
The house is nice. **Its** garden is big.
We're painting a poster for **our** school.
Mr and Mrs Ahmed are in **their** shop.

G

Asif and Dave, what's your idea?

Let's have a wet sponge stall …

… with pupils – and teachers!

Oh no!

STORY

Come to the wet sponge stall! Asif and Dave's stall is lots of fun.
– But is their stall fun for Mrs Brown?

Only a false alarm

ASIF	Thank you, Pete. You're very wet!
DAVE	Hey, look! Mrs Brown is coming now.
ASIF	Come to the wet sponge stall, Mrs Brown.
DAVE	It's lots of fun.
5 **MRS BROWN**	It's lots of fun for you. OK.
ASIF	Come to the wet sponge stall!
	Bring your money!
	Throw a wet sponge at a teacher!
SHARON	Mrs Brown, Mrs Brown!
10 **MRS BROWN**	What's the matter, Sharon?
SHARON	Is your car a red *Cortino*?
MRS BROWN	Yes, it is.
SHARON	Its alarm is on. Let's go to your car.

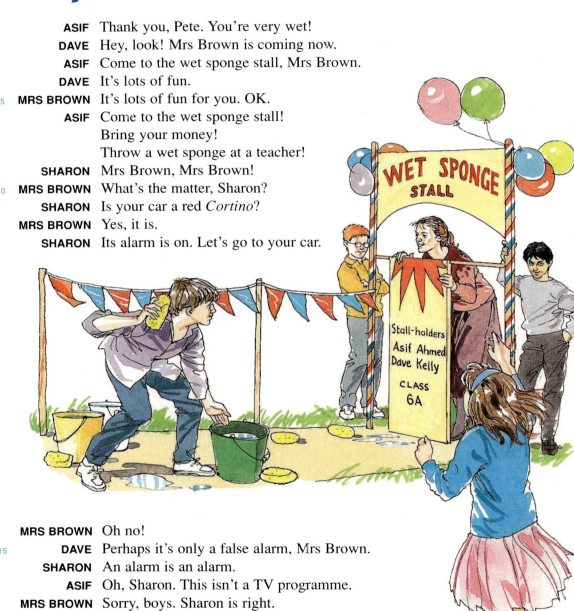

MRS BROWN	Oh no!
15 **DAVE**	Perhaps it's only a false alarm, Mrs Brown.
SHARON	An alarm is an alarm.
ASIF	Oh, Sharon. This isn't a TV programme.
MRS BROWN	Sorry, boys. Sharon is right.
	I'm going to my car – now.

20 Sharon, Asif and Dave are standing with Mrs Brown.
But they aren't standing at the wet sponge stall now.
They're standing next to Mrs Brown's car.

MRS BROWN	Yes, it's only a false alarm.
SHARON	I'm very sorry, Mrs Brown.
25 **MRS BROWN**	It's OK, Sharon. And thank you.
	The wet sponge stall is terrible.
ASIF	Oh, yes, the wet sponge stall!
MRS BROWN	Sorry, boys. It's too late.
	There are other jobs for me now.
30 **ASIF**	Oh no!
DAVE	Your car alarm is terrible,
	Mrs Brown.
MRS BROWN	You're right, Dave.
	But today it's a
35	very good alarm.

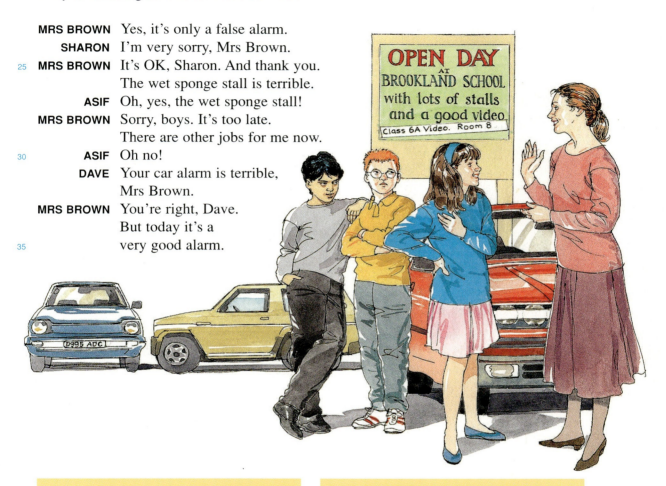

OPEN DAY
AT
BROOKLAND SCHOOL
with lots of stalls
and a good video
Class 6A Video. Room 8

D995 ADC

TASK A ■ One word is wrong.

1 It's Sharon and Dave's stall.
2 Sharon is very wet.
3 Throw a wet book at pupils and teachers.
4 Mrs Brown's alarm is a red *Cortino*.
5 Sharon, Claire and Asif are standing with Mrs Brown.
6 The alarm is terrible for Mrs Brown today.

TASK B ■ What are the right words?

car alarm · false alarm · fun
jobs · open day · stall

1 It's the Brookland School …
2 Dave and Asif are at their …
3 It's lots of … for pupils.
4 Mrs Brown's … is on.
5 But it's only a …
6 There are lots of … for Mrs Brown.

W 6-8

ACTIVE ENGLISH

ACTIONS 🎧 Vorschläge machen

In der Schule: Was schlägt Karen vor?

KAREN	Let's watch a video, Mrs Hill.
MRS HILL	Sorry, not today, Karen. Open your books, please.
KAREN	Oh, OK.

Nach der Schule: Ist Ben mit dem Vorschlag einverstanden?

HANNAH	Let's ride our bikes.
BEN	No, not now.
HANNAH	Are you busy?
BEN	Yes, I am. I'm painting a poster.

EXERCISE ■ **What are your ideas for the afternoon? Make some dialogues.**

YOU

Let's	listen to	our bikes.
	go	a video.
	read	your new CD.
	ride	to a computer shop.
	watch	a football match.
	have	a comic.

A PARTNER

- Good idea!
- Super. Let's go.
- Sorry. I'm busy.
- Oh, OK.
- Not now.

W 9-10

CLASS PROJECT An open day for your class

Make posters for stalls at an open day.
book stall ▪ cake stall ▪ CD stall ▪ comic stall
plant stall ▪ sweet stall ▪ video stall

Some words:
- bring   ▪ come
- have   ▪ listen to
- make   ▪ read

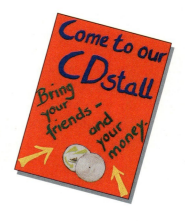

44

ACTIVITY Write a postcard.

Here are some postcards from pupils at an English school.

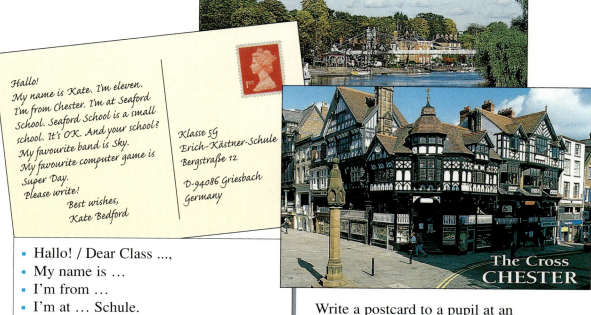

Hallo!
My name is Kate. I'm eleven.
I'm from Chester. I'm at Seaford
School. Seaford School is a small
school. It's OK. And your school?
My favourite band is Sky.
My favourite computer game is
Super Day.
Please write!
  Best wishes,
    Kate Bedford

Klasse 5G
Erich-Kästner-Schule
Bergstraße 12

D-94086 Griesbach
Germany

The Cross
CHESTER

- Hallo! / Dear Class ...,
- My name is …
- I'm from …
- I'm at … Schule.
- My favourite band/game / TV show is …
- Best wishes, …

Write a postcard to a pupil at an
English school.

LOOK AROUND YOU English is "in".

Kinder und Jugendliche in Deutschland verwenden oft englische
Wörter. Welche englischen Wörter benutzt du?

War das ein schlechter
Joke, Mann!

Bist du auch in
Florians Team?

Echt cool.

OK. Let's go!

Im Internet
Surfen ist irre!

KLASSE 5A

Dein neues T-Shirt
finde ich super!

Wir haben Tickets für das
Open-Air-Konzert gekriegt!

Das ist
doch easy!

PRACTICE PAGES

STRUCTURES

EXERCISE 1 ■ Posters

Come ▪ Listen to ▪ Read ▪ Ride ▪ Watch ▪ Write

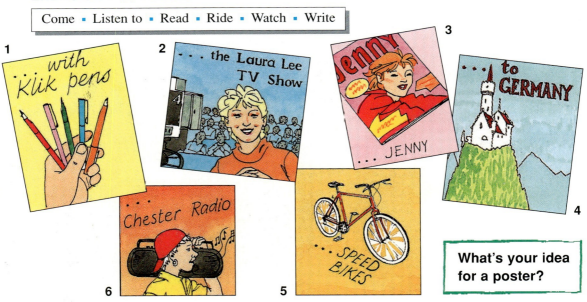

What's your idea for a poster?

EXERCISE 2 ■ What are their ideas for the evening?

1 Let's watch …
2 Let's go …
3 Let's ride …
4 Let's listen to …
5 Let's paint …
6 Let's read …

a poster ▪ a video ▪ our bikes
some cassettes ▪ some comics ▪ to the bike shop

EXERCISE 3 ■ Not at the open day!

My ▪ your ▪ his ▪ her
Our ▪ their

1 **ASIF** I'm sorry. … parents are busy, Mrs Brown.
2 **SHARON AND CLAIRE** Oh no! … poster is at home.
3 **MRS DALE** Mark and Tom are with … dad in Manchester.
4 **MRS BROWN** Pete, where's … sign?
5 **TARIQ** My dad is with … football team.
6 **PETE** Pat? She isn't here. She's with … friends. W 11-13

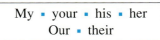

SITUATIONS

Was sagst du auf Englisch, wenn …

1 … du jemanden aufforderst zuzuhören? (Do this, please. / Listen, please.)
2 … du jemanden aufforderst sich hinzusetzen? (Stand up, please. / Sit down, please.)
3 … du jemandem dankst? (Thank you. / You're very good.)
4 … du fragst, ob jemand beschäftigt ist? (Are you at home? / Are you busy?)
5 … du einem Vorschlag nicht zustimmst? (No, not now. / Yes, OK.)
6 … du einem Vorschlag zustimmst? (Sorry. I'm busy. / Good idea!)

Tipp: Alle Sätze findest du auf den Seiten 38-44.

WORDPOWER

WORDPOWER 1 ■ Make two groups.

> board ▪ bring ▪ chair ▪ class ▪ come
> cupboard ▪ go ▪ listen ▪ make ▪ open day
> pupil ▪ read ▪ ride ▪ table ▪ teacher ▪ watch

1 Things at school: board, …
2 Actions: bring, …

WORDPOWER 2 ■ From Sally Parks in England to Karin Koßler in Germany

> at ▪ Class ▪ fun ▪ money ▪ open
> stalls ▪ teacher ▪ Throw ▪ wet

I'm … King School here in England. I'm in … 6B. My … is Mrs Taylor. There's an … day at our school. There are lots of … The … is for the new school minibus. There's a … sponge stall, too. It's lots of … "… a wet sponge at a teacher or pupil." Super!

Bye,
Sally

WORDPOWER 3 ■ Car and minibus

- car
- stand up
- come
- morning
- table
- door
- poster
- teacher

- afternoon
- go
- chair
- minibus
- sign
- pupil
- sit down
- window

W 14-16

SOUNDS 🎧

Ben's pens …

[b]: bag, big, boy, board, but, Bob, job, rubber
[p]: pen, open, parents, Pat, up, group, shop, put

SPECIAL TOPIC

Colours

What's your favourite colour? Is it …?

red   blue   yellow   green   black   white   brown   pink

EXERCISE 1 ■ **What colour is the …?**

1 What colour is the house? – *Pink.*
2 What colour is the phone?
3 What colour is the sign?
4 What colour is the number plate?

5 What colour is the bus?
6 What colour is the taxi?
7 What colour is the bike?
8 What colours are the jelly babies?

EXERCISE 2 ■ **What colour is your …?**

1 What colour is your board?
2 What colour is your sweatshirt?
3 What colour is your bag?

4 What colour is your pen?
5 What colour is your English book?
6 What colour is your phone at home?

W 17-18

SONG 🎧 Balloons are over our town

Verse 1
Red, green, yellow, blue,
Brown, white, pink
Balloons are over our town.
Red, green, yellow, blue,
Brown, white, **POP**!
One balloon is down, down, down.

Verse 7
Red, green, yellow, blue,
Brown, white, pink
Balloons are over our town.
POP, **POP**, **POP**, **POP**,
POP, POP, **POP**!
All balloons are down, down, down.

Verse 2
Red, green, yellow, blue,
Brown, white, pink
Balloons are over our town.
Red, green, yellow, blue
Brown, POP, **POP**!
Two balloons are down, down, down.

Verses 3-6

LISTENING 🎧 What colour is it?

Right or wrong?

1 Jenny's bike is blue.
2 The black bag is next to the door.
3 Martin is from Green Road.

4 Mark's favourite jelly babies are green.
5 The cake is for Tom.

W 19-21

SUMMARY

There's a … / There are some …

Damit kannst du sagen, was vorhanden ist oder was es gibt.

There's a dog in the garden

Eine Sache:

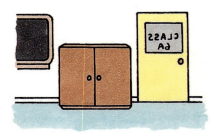

Mehrere Sachen:

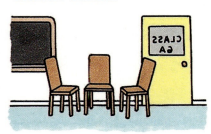

There's a cupboard in the classroom.   There are some chairs in the classroom.

There's a car in the garage. Es ist ein Auto in der Garage.
There are some cakes in the kitchen. In der Küche gibt es einige Kuchen.

…, please.

Manchmal willst du jemanden auffordern, etwas zu tun.

Come here, please. Komm bitte hierher.
Write your name, please. Schreib bitte deinen Namen.
Bring some comics, please. Bringt bitte einige Comics mit.
Please go to your car. Gehen Sie bitte zu Ihrem Auto.

Nützliche Verben (*verbs*) für Aufforderungen:
bring · come · do · go · listen · make
open · paint · read · sit down · watch · write

Let's sit down.

Let's …

Mit *Let's* … kannst du jemandem vorschlagen,
dass ihr etwas gemeinsam tut.

Let's go. Gehen wir.
Let's watch the video. Sehen wir uns doch das Video an.
Let's read our comics. Lass/Lasst uns unsere Comics lesen.

my, your, his, ...

Solche Wörter zeigen, wem etwas gehört.

Where's my pencil?

	I	you	he	she	it	we	you	they
Possessivform	**my**	**your**	**his**	**her**	**its**	**our**	**your**	**their**

Boris is Dave's cat. Boris is his cat. Boris ist Daves Katze. Boris ist seine Katze.
Terry is Sharon's dog. Terry is her dog. Terry ist Sharons Hund. Terry ist ihr Hund.
The house is small, but its garage is big. Das Haus ist klein, aber seine Garage ist groß.
We're in Class 6A. Here's our teacher. Wir sind in Klasse 6A. Hier ist unsere Lehrerin.

IN DIESER UNIT HAST DU GELERNT, ...

... zu sagen, was vorhanden ist oder was es gibt. ➡ There's a flat above the shop.
There are some books in the bag.

... jemanden aufzufordern, etwas zu tun. ➡ Sit down, please.

... Vorschläge zu machen. ➡ Let's ride our bikes.

... auf Vorschläge zu reagieren. ➡ Good idea!
Sorry. I'm busy.

... zu fragen, welche Farbe etwas hat. ➡ What colour is the pen?

DU KANNST AUCH VERSTEHEN, WIE...

... gesagt wird, was jemand gerade tut. ➡ Pete is planning a stall.
Some girls are making a video.
I'm painting a poster.

... gesagt wird, was jemand im Moment nicht tut. ➡ They aren't standing at the wet sponge stall now.

UNIT FOUR
I'm hungry! 🎧

A

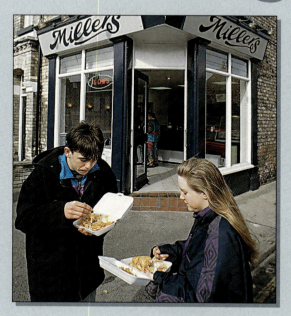

The children are hungry.
They're eating fish and chips.
It's a cheap take-away meal.
It's from a chip shop.

Take-away food in your town		
There's a	restaurant snack bar stall	in … Straße.
They have	good terrible very nice cheap	meals. snacks.

B

Hamburger restaurants have take-away meals, too.
They have hamburgers, cheeseburgers, chips and other food.
And they have milk shakes and other drinks.

EXERCISE 1 ■ **Food and drinks at *Burger World***

They have hamburgers.
They have chips.
They have …   W 1

Burger World

hamburgers

chips

milk shakes

cola

hot dogs

cheeseburgers

C

SHARON	I'm hungry.
DAVE	What about a snack?
SHARON	Are your mother and father at home?
DAVE	No, but *my* snacks are great.
	What's in the kitchen?
	Look, we have lots of things:

burgers

rolls

ketchup

cheese

EXERCISE 2 ■ Dave's idea for a snack

DAVE	Great! Let's make cheeseburgers.
	We have burgers.
	We have …
	We …

D

SHARON	I'm thirsty.
	What about lemonade?
DAVE	Lemonade?
	Sorry. I don't have lemonade.

EXERCISE 3 ■ Make dialogues with a partner. You don't have the things.

1 orange juice
2 apple juice
3 cola
4 *Sprint*   W 2

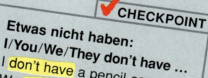

We don't have lemonade.
But we have a bottle of milk.
We have a carton of ice-cream.
Let's make a Dave Kelly
milk shake!

E Dave has bananas.
He has ice-cream.
He has chocolate.
He has milk.
He has the things for chocolate or banana milk shakes.

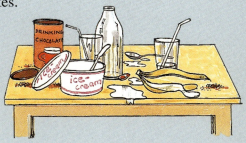

F

SHARON	Your milk shake is good, Dave.
	Now let's watch *Australian Friends* on TV.
DAVE	We don't have cable TV.
SHARON	Our house has cable TV.
DAVE	OK. Let's go!

EXERCISE 4 ■ **What are their meals for school?**

Asif has a sandwich.
He has yoghurt.
And he has cola.

Sharon has a cheese roll.
She has crisps.
And she has …

Claire has …
She has …
And she has …

Pat …
She …
And she …

Dave …
He …
…

> **✔ CHECKPOINT**
>
> **Etwas haben:**
> **He/She/It has …**
> Sue <mark>has</mark> a banana.
> And Alan?
> – He <mark>has</mark> an apple.

What's your snack for school?
What's in your bag?
– I have a snack in my bag. I have …
– I don't have a snack.

W 3

G

Adam is at home now.
He's hungry and thirsty.
He has some empty cartons.
But he doesn't have a snack.
And he doesn't have a drink.

EXERCISE 5 ■ Adam doesn't have …

Adam doesn't have burgers. He doesn't have …

EXERCISE 6 ■ Claire has a TV. She doesn't have a radio.

1 Claire has a TV.
She doesn't have a radio.

2 Dave has a …
He doesn't have a …

3 Sharon has …
She …

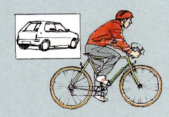

4 Mr Hill …
He …

5 Asif …
He …

6 Mrs Brown …
She …

✔ **CHECKPOINT**

Etwas nicht haben:
He/She/It doesn't have …
She doesn't have a pen.
He doesn't have the money.
It doesn't have a garden.

And your friend?
My friend has a …
He/She doesn't have a …

W 4

STORY 🎧

Mrs Kelly was ill. Dave had an idea for a surprise …

The surprise meal

Claire was at Dave and Adam's house.
They had Dave's new drink – a *Brown Cow*.

"This is great," Claire said.
"Your brother's hobby is good, Adam.
5 His snacks and drinks are super."
    "But Dave is always in the kitchen," Adam said.
"Your hobby is good, Claire. Bikes are fun.
Let's go. Let's ride our bikes now."
    "No, I have an idea," Dave said.
10 "Dad isn't at home. And mum is in the bedroom. She's ill.
Let's make a surprise meal."
    "Oh, no!" Adam said.
Claire said, "Oh, it's very late. Er, my friends
are coming to our house. Bye."
15   "Yes, let's go, Claire," Adam said.
    "*You* have some jobs here, Adam," Dave said.
    "But I'm not good at cooking."
    "Well, put the things on the table and wash up."

After fifty minutes …

20 Dave's surprise meal was very good.
It was spaghetti with different sauces.
And he had American chocolate cakes.
But Adam had lots of jobs.

The meal was a big surprise for Mr Kelly.
25 But there was a surprise for Dave and Adam, too.
Mr Kelly had a bag.
It was fish and chips from the chip shop.
– Now the Kellys had *two* surprise meals.

TASK A ■ **Right or wrong?**
1 Claire was at Asif's flat.
2 The *Brown Cow* was terrible.
3 Mr Kelly was ill.
4 Mrs Kelly was at home.
5 Dave's meal was fish and chips.
6 Adam had lots of jobs.
7 Mr Kelly had a surprise meal, too.

TASK B ■ ■ **What's Dave saying to his mum?**

have / don't have ▪ has / doesn't have

1 Dad … a surprise for you.
2 Adam and I … a surprise, too.
3 We … two meals.
4 We … only one meal.
5 I … spaghetti.
6 I … some chocolate cakes, too.
7 Dad … chocolate cakes.
8 He only … fish and chips.

MRS KELLY But I'm ill. I'm not hungry.

W 5-6

ACTIVE ENGLISH

ACTIONS 🎧 Familien beschreiben

Who is it?
Hallo. Here's my family.
My father's name is Derek.
My mother's name is Jean.
They have three children – a daughter
and two sons.
I have two brothers. I don't have a sister.
Who am I?

Who isn't in the photo? Why not?
I'm Pete.
The photo is at my aunt and uncle's house.
I have a brother and a sister.
I have a dog.
He's in the photo, too.
Where's my brother, Grant?
He has the camera!

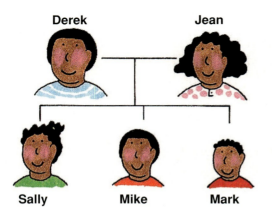

Derek   Jean

Sally   Mike   Mark

EXERCISE ■ **Asif's family**

ASIF   Here's my family.
I have a mother.
I have …

And your family?

I have	a father.
	a mother.
	a brother / … brothers.
	a sister / … sisters.
	a grandmother / two grandmothers.
	a grandfather / two grandfathers.
	an aunt / … aunts.
	an uncle / … uncles.

His/Her name is … / Their names are …

I don't have a/an …

W 7-8

4

ACTIVITY A family tree

Make your family tree.
Write the names.
Who are they?

ACTIVITY Dave's chocolate crispies

1 Put chocolate (100g) in a big dish.

2 Melt it with hot water, or in a microwave.

3 Put in some cornflakes (75g) and mix.

4 Make small cakes.

5 Eat them when they're cold.

It's my favourite snack!

And Dave's *Brown Cow*?
Put vanilla ice-cream in a glass with cola. Great!

LOOK AROUND YOU American food

★ Make a poster about American food and drinks in Germany.

★ Write about an American restaurant in Germany.

- … has American food.
- It's / It isn't very popular.
- They have …
- Their food is/isn't nicer than German food.

PRACTICE PAGES

STRUCTURES

EXERCISE 1 ■ Sharon and Asif

	Sharon	Asif
TV	✔	
computer		✔
walkman	✔	
football	✔	✔
bike	✔	✔
dog	✔	
football poster		✔

Sharon has a TV.
She doesn't have a computer.
She has a walkman.
She …

Asif doesn't have a TV.
He has a …

> **And you?**
> I have a …   I don't have a …

EXERCISE 2 ■ What's in your bag and pencil-case?

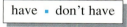

1 I … a red pen.
2 I … a blue pencil.
3 I … a drink.
4 I … a sandwich.
5 … a comic.
6 … an apple.
7 … a maths book.
8 … a ruler.

EXERCISE 3 ■■ It isn't right!

1 Adam has a car.
  – *No! Adam doesn't have a car.*

2 Mr and Mrs Ahmed have a restaurant.
  – *No! Mr and Mrs Ahmed don't have …*
3 Sharon has a bike in her bed.
4 Cats have lots of money.
5 A school has lots of dogs.
6 Dave has a pink cat.
7 Comics have exercises.
8 Terry and Boris have phones.

EXERCISE 4 ■ Claire is at Asif's flat. Write a word with 's.

1 Our family has a big flat.
  Our *family's* flat is above the shop.
2 My grandmother is in her bedroom.
  My … bedroom is next to my bedroom.
3 Aysha has good CDs.
  … CDs are here.

4 Aysha is my sister.
  Aysha is my … name.
5 There's Bina.
  … room is here.
6 This computer game is from a friend.
  It's a … game.

W 9-10

SITUATIONS

Wie sagst du auf Englisch, dass …

1 … du Hunger hast?
2 … du Durst hast?
3 … etwas toll ist?

4 … du eine Idee hast?
5 … es sehr spät ist?
6 … du keine Schwester hast?

Tipp: Alle Sätze findest du auf den Seiten 52-58.

WORDPOWER

WORDPOWER 1 ■ What's the meal?

WORDPOWER 2 ■ Five family words

One word isn't a family word!

WORDPOWER 3 ■ Who? Where?

1 … are the boys? – My brothers.
2 … are your friends? – At school.
3 …'s their teacher? – Mrs Brown.
4 … are you from? England?

5 …'s my bike?
6 … are you? Tim?
7 … are my cakes?
8 …'s in the garden?

WORDPOWER 4 ■ Ordne die Wörter der Größe nach.

1 road • town • shop • room
room, shop, road, town
2 pencil-case • pen • bag • classroom
3 chair • house • flat • bedroom
4 Europe • Elm Road • Chester • England
5 fifteen • five • fifty • forty • four
6 kitchen • meal • restaurant • snack

W 11-12

WORDPOWER 5 ■ Black and white

1 black	4 sister	7 great
2 big	5 new	8 parents
3 go	6 food	9 hallo

brother	goodbye	old
children	drink	small
come	terrible	white

SOUNDS 🎧

[g]: good, garden, green, girl, big, bag, dog
[k]: car, comic, book, pink, make, cake
[g]-[k]: a good car, a black bag, a big cake

SPECIAL TOPIC

Money

There are 100 pence (p) in a pound (£).

45p	forty-five p [pi:], forty-five pence
£1	a pound
£1.25	one pound twenty-five
£2	two pounds
£5.80	five pounds eighty

EXERCISE 1 ■ **In a shop: Make dialogues.**

Dialogue a

YOU How much is the calculator?
A PARTNER It's £8.45.

calculator £8.45

Dialogue b

YOU Can I have this calculator, please?
A PARTNER £8.45, please.

pen £5.20

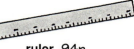

ruler 94p

badge £2.20

postcard 60p

book £8.40

magazine £2.50

EMMA My pocket-money is £3 a week.

PETE £3 a week! You're lucky.
My pocket-money is only £7 a month.

> My pocket-money
> is €… a month/a week/…

€0.50	fifty cents
€1.00	a euro / one euro
€1.10	one euro ten
€2.00	two euros
€3.40	three euros forty

EXERCISE 2 ■ **Things in German shops**

YOU How much is a *Flax* comic / …?

A PARTNER It's €2.50. / …

YOU You're right. / No, it's €…

W 13-14

POEM 🎧 Hot cross buns

Hot cross buns,
Hot cross buns,
One a penny,
Two a penny,
Hot cross buns.

If you have no daughters,
Give them to your sons,
One a penny,
Two a penny,
Hot cross buns.

LISTENING 🎧 How much is it?

1 Where are the children? Listen.

> At school. ▪ In a bike shop.
> In a restaurant. ▪ In a shop.

2 Right or wrong? Listen.

1 Simon's chocolate is 50p.
2 *Beano* and *Dandy* are sweets.
3 Simon's things are £1.40.

4 *Maxi Cola* is 90p.
5 *Great Girl* is £2.
6 The girl has a cola and a comic.

W 15-16

SUMMARY

have

Mit *have/has* kannst du sagen, was jemand besitzt oder hat.

You have two ice-creams!
I don't have an ice-cream.

We have new cameras.

Tina has a dog.

We don't have a calculator.

We have a cat. Wir haben eine Katze.
We don't have a dog. Wir haben keinen Hund.
Mrs Kelly has the car today. Heute hat Frau Kelly das Auto.
Mr Kelly doesn't have the car today. Herr Kelly hat das Auto heute nicht.

AUSSAGEN

I You We You They	have a nice room.

Nach *I/you/we/they* verwendest du *have*.

He (Dave) She (Sharon) It (The house)	has a big garden.

Nach *he/she/it* verwendest du *has*.

VERNEINUNGEN

I You ――― We You They	don't have a garden.

Nach *I/you/we/they* verwendest du die Form *don't have*.

Die Langform von *don't have* ist *do not have*.

He (Mr Reed) She (Mrs Fox) It (The house)	doesn't have a garden.

Nach *he/she/it* verwendest du die Form *doesn't have*.

Die Langform von *doesn't have* ist *does not have*.

I don't have a computer. Ich habe keinen Computer.
We don't have a car. Wir haben kein Auto.
My sister doesn't have a bike. Meine Schwester hat kein Fahrrad.
Dad doesn't have a hamburger. Vati hat keinen Hamburger.   Tipp: Fragen lernst du in Unit 6.

IN DIESER UNIT HAST DU GELERNT, ...

... zu sagen, dass du Hunger oder Durst hast. ➡ *I'm hungry.*
I'm thirsty.

... zu sagen, dass du etwas besitzt/hast. ➡ *I have a good bike.*

... zu sagen, dass du etwas nicht besitzt/hast. ➡ *I don't have a red pen.*

... über die Familie zu sprechen. ➡ *I have a sister.*
I don't have an uncle.

... über Geld und Preise zu sprechen. ➡ *How much is this pen?*
It's £1.50.

... im Geschäft um etwas zu bitten. ➡ *Can I have this pen, please?*

DU KANNST AUCH VERSTEHEN, ...

... wie Mengenangaben gemacht werden. ➡ *a bottle of milk*

UNIT FIVE
Buy my toys!

A

This is a car-boot sale. It's in a field near a town.
There are lots of cheap things at car-boot sales – new or second-hand. The things are in car-boots or on tables. Car-boot sales are very popular in England. There are always lots of people. Claire and her mother are often at car-boot sales at the weekend.

B At a car-boot sale there are toys. There are walkmans. There are …

toys   **walkmans**   **books**   **CDs**   **tools**

pictures   **games**   **comics**

> **In Germany
> there are markets
> with second-hand …**

C **MRS HALL** I go to car-boot sales near Chester.
I go with Claire.
We meet my sister there.
We buy lots of things.
We eat a snack, too.

EXERCISE 1 ■ **And Claire?**

CLAIRE		
	1 I go	lots of fun there.
	2 I eat	to car-boot sales.
	3 I buy	some friends there.
	4 I meet	comics and games.
	5 I have	a snack, too.

W 1

1 I go to car-boot sales.
2 I eat …

66   I go

D

My walkman is broken. And I have no money.

You have lots of old toys and comics. Sell them at a car-boot sale.

Good idea! Money for a walkman. And let's help the animal home, too.

E What's in Sharon's toy cupboard? She has a train. She has a …

train　　　building set　　　doll　　　farm set　　　football

game　　　car　　　kite

And you?
I have a …
I don't have a …

F Sharon has a big bag for the car-boot sale.

SHARON　I play with this train.
CLAIRE　OK. Leave it in the cupboard.
SHARON　But I don't play with this car.
CLAIRE　Good. Put it in the bag.
SHARON　And I don't play with this doll.

EXERCISE 2 ■ Sharon's toys

I play with … (✔) ▪ I don't play with … (✘)

SHARON　　I play with the train. (✔)
　　　　I don't play with the car. (✘)
　　　　　　… the doll. (✘)
　　　　　　… the farm set. (✔)
　　　　　　… the football. (✘)
　　　　　　… the game. (✘)
　　　　… the building set. (✘)
　　　　　　… the kite. (✔)

✔ **CHECKPOINT**

Gewohnheiten
So sagst du, was du nicht tust:
I don't read comics.
I don't watch Sesame Street.
I don't play with dolls.

W 2-3

G Sharon has some old comics for the car-boot sale.
Children in England read lots of different comics.

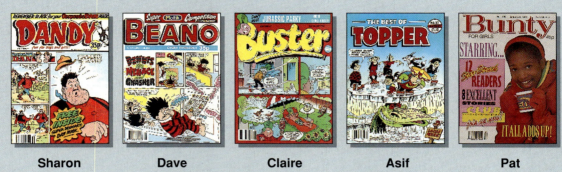

| Sharon | Dave | Claire | Asif | Pat |

Sharon reads *Dandy*. Dave reads *Beano*. Claire …

EXERCISE 3 ■ Some people in comics

1 Ball Boy
2 Dennis
3 Bananaman
4 Dan
5 Vid Kid
6 Billy Whizz

Ball Boy plays	lots of things.
Dennis breaks	lots of videos.
Bananaman helps	big meals.
Dan eats	people.
Vid Kid watches	from place to place.
Billy Whizz runs	football.

1 Ball Boy plays football.
2 Dennis …

H Sharon has comics for the car-boot sale. She has some toys, too.
She doesn't play with the toys.

Sharon doesn't play with the doll.
She doesn't play with the game.
She doesn't play with …
She doesn't play …
She doesn't …

EXERCISE 4 ■ **Sharon's brother is only 2. Kevin doesn't read comics.**

buy · play · read · ride · watch · write

1 He doesn't … *Pop Show* on TV.
2 He doesn't … football.
3 He doesn't … CDs.
4 He doesn't … comics.
5 He doesn't … a bike.
6 He doesn't … exercises.

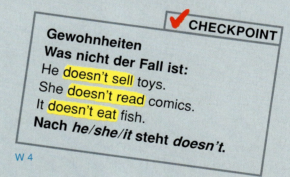

✔ **CHECKPOINT**

Gewohnheiten
Was nicht der Fall ist:
He doesn't sell toys.
She doesn't read comics.
It doesn't eat fish.
Nach *he/she/it* steht *doesn't*.

W 4

I Sharon is with her mother.

STORY 🎧

Sharon needs money. The animal home needs money, too.

A special customer

Sharon and Claire are at the car-boot sale.

SHARON Here are Dave and Asif.
Hallo, you two. I have a very
good football here. It costs £1.
5 ASIF That's too expensive for us!
What about 70p?
SHARON 70p? Hmm, 80p.
DAVE OK.
CLAIRE The football has a good name.
10 ASIF Oh no! *Manchester City Special!*

Later …

CLAIRE We don't have enough money.
But it's very late.
People are going.
SHARON Let's put the things in the bag. 15
MAN Excuse me. How much is this doll?
CLAIRE It costs £4. Very cheap.
MAN My wife collects dolls.
SHARON It's a *Dinky* doll.
MAN OK. Here's £4. Is this your first 20
car-boot sale?
SHARON Yes, it is. I want money for a new
walkman. And I want money for the
animal home, too.
MAN I come here every week 25
and I sell walkmans at my stall.
SHARON How much are they?
MAN I have some cheap walkmans for
only £8.50. They have batteries, too.
SHARON I don't have £8.50. I only have £7. 30
CLAIRE And it's very late now. Let's go.

70

Sharon and Claire are leaving the car-boot sale.

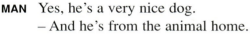

CLAIRE	Look, over there. That's the man with the walkmans again.
MAN	Hallo. My wife likes the doll. Thank you.
35	What about a good walkman now? They're only £8.50.
SHARON	Yes, they're very nice. But I only have £7.
MAN	OK, £5.
	That's a special price for a special customer.
	And you have £2 for the animal home.
40	You like animals and I like animals, too.
SHARON	That's great! Thank you.
MAN	Here's my dog, Jacko.
CLAIRE	He's very friendly. I like him.
MAN	Yes, he's a very nice dog.
45	– And he's from the animal home.

TASK A ■ Right or wrong?

1 £1 is too expensive for Asif and Dave.
2 Asif likes the name on the football.
3 The man collects dolls.
4 The doll costs £5.
5 The man sells cassettes.
6 The man's dog is in an animal home.

TASK B ■ ■ The man at the car-boot sale

1 walkmans/He/at his stall/sells
   He sells walkmans at his stall.
2 comes/to the car-boot sale/ every week/He
3 cost/His/walkmans/£8.50
4 animals/dogs/likes/He/other/and
5 the animal home/a dog/He/has/from

W 5-6

ACTIVE ENGLISH

ACTIONS 🎧 Sagen, was man mag

Mögen Tina und Lucy die gleichen Sendungen?

TINA   What's your favourite programme?
LUCY   *The Music Show.*
TINA   I like *Sports Time*.
LUCY   I don't like that programme. It's terrible.

Wer mag das Sweatshirt nicht?

NICK   I like your sweatshirt.
PETE   My sweatshirt?
NICK   Yes, it's very nice.
PETE   I don't like it. Yellow isn't my favourite colour.

EXERCISE 🟥 **What are your favourite things?**

YOU   … is my favourite …
A PARTNER   – I like …, too.
   – I don't like …
   … is my favourite …

magazine

book/film/…

pop group

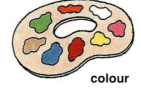

colour

TV programme

CD

sport

game

W 7-8

72

POEMS 🎧 Some favourite things

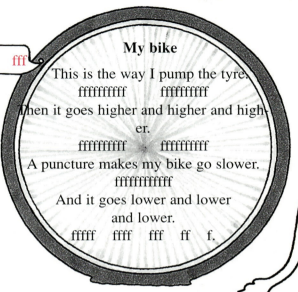

My bike

This is the way I pump the tyre.
fffffffff   fffffffff
Then it goes higher and higher and higher.
fffffffff   fffffffff
A puncture makes my bike go slower.
fffffffffff
And it goes lower and lower
and lower.
fffff   ffff   fff   ff   f.

Ice-cream
I scream,
You scream.
We all scream
For ice-cream.

The cow
The friendly cow all red and white
I love with all my heart.
She gives me cream with all her might
To eat with apple tart.   R.L. Stevenson

CLASS PROJECT Write about your favourite stars.

Here's Al Burton. He's my favourite singer. I think he's great. He's American. I like all his songs. My favourite song is "Our town". I have lots of his CDs. I have lots of photos of him, too.

- Here's …
- He's/She's my favourite | singer.
  film star.
  TV star.
  …
- I think he's/she's great.
- He's/She's American/German/…
- I like all his/her songs/films/…
- My favourite … is …
- I have lots of his/her CDs/videos.
- I have lots of photos of him/her.

LOOK AROUND YOU Music

- What are your favourite songs?
  Are they in English or in German?
- Look at a pop magazine and find some English words.

PRACTICE PAGES

STRUCTURES

EXERCISE 1 ■ What's right?

I (leave/leaves) the house with my sister.
A bus (go/goes) to our school.
Jill and I (eat/eats) at school.
I (have/has) sandwiches from home.

Jill (eat/eats) a school meal.
We (leave/leaves) in the afternoon.
Dad (make/makes) our evening meal.
I (watch/watches) videos in the evening.

EXERCISE 2 ■ Mr Low and Mrs Lee

a Mr Low

1 My children (not help) at home.
   My children *don't help* at home.
2 They (not wash up) after meals.
3 They (not read) their books for school.
4 They (not play) with the dog.
5 And they (not like) my meals!

b Mrs Lee

1 My Joe (not like) games.
   My Joe *doesn't like* games.
2 He (not have) nice friends.
3 He (not eat) his meals.
4 He (not play) with the cat.
   He's a terrible dog!

EXERCISE 3 ■■ Oh, this terrible toy-shop!

1 The trains … go.
2 The doll … stand up.
3 The cats … sit down.

don't does-n't

4 The pens … write.
5 The walkman … play.
6 The dog … run.

EXERCISE 4 ■ Here and over there

This is ▪ That's

1

… my bike, over there.

2

… my cat.

3

… our house.

4

… our new car.

5

… my kite, over there.

W 9

74

SITUATIONS

Wie sagst du auf Englisch, dass …

1 … du dir Videos anschaust?
2 … dein Walkman kaputt ist?
3 … du keine Comics liest?

4 … etwas £1 kostet?
5 … ihr nicht genug Geld habt?
6 … du etwas nicht magst?

Tip: Look again at pages 66-72.

WORDPOWER

WORDPOWER 1 ■ A car-boot sale

after ▪ at ▪ in ▪ near ▪ to ▪ with

1 Sharon is … Aysha.
2 "I'm going … a car-boot sale."
3 "Lots of people are … the car-boot sale."
4 "The car-boot sale is … a field."
5 "The field is … our town, in Stockwell."
6 "Come to our house … the car-boot sale."

WORDPOWER 3 ■ Eric's market stall

bring ▪ buy ▪ come ▪ leave ▪ sell ▪ watch

1 I … to the market here every day.
2 I … sweets.
3 I … the sweets in my car.
4 Lots of children … sweets from my stall.
5 I … the market late.
6 In the evenings? I … *Market Street* on TV.

WORDPOWER 2 ■ At a car-boot sale: Find 10 words.

buy ▪ cat ▪ cheap ▪ customer
daughter ▪ expensive ▪ field ▪ house
lesson ▪ money ▪ price ▪ programme
second-hand ▪ sell ▪ sister ▪ stall

WORDPOWER 4 ■ What's the right word?

1 My dad (rides/reads) lots of books.

2 The book (comes/costs) £5.
3 I (watch/wash) up in the evenings.
4 Tom (makes/meets) great cakes.
5 They (start/sell) nice things at the shop.
6 Bill (buys/brings) toys at a toy-shop.

W 10-13

SOUNDS 🎧

[s]: sister, sale, seven, snack, stand, poster, cost
[ʃ]: Sharon, shop, she, English, fish, sweatshirt
[tʃ]: Chester, cheap, children, chair, chocolate, watch, teacher

Cheap chocolate from Chester!

SPECIAL TOPIC

The time

a It's two o'clock.   It's four o'clock.   It's six o'clock.

b It's five ten.   It's nine thirty.   It's seven forty-five.

c It's seven o nine.   It's three o six.   It's twelve fifty-three.

EXERCISE 1 ■ What time is it?

EXERCISE 2 ■ Let's go to Woodlake! But when?

LUCY   **HANIF**   **MIKE**   **SALLY**   **TINA**

Let's go at 10 o'clock.   No. Let's go at …   …   …   …

W 14-15

POEM 🎧 Hickory dickory dock

Hickory, dickory, dock,
The mouse ran up the clock.
The clock struck one,
The mouse ran down.
Hickory, dickory, dock.

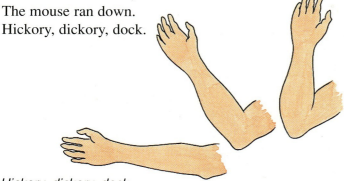

Hickory, dickory, dock,

The mouse ran up the clock.

The clock struck one,

The mouse ran down.

LISTENING 🎧 The time

1 Where are the people? Listen.

At a car-boot sale. (2x) ▪ At home. ▪ At school. (2x)

Dialogue 1: …   Dialogue 2: …   Dialogue 3: …   Dialogue 4: …   Dialogue 5: …

2 What time ...? Listen.
Dialogue 1: What time is it?
Dialogue 2: What time is it now?
Dialogue 3: When's Mrs Bakewell's lesson?
Dialogue 4: When's the TV programme?
Dialogue 5: What time is it?

W 16-17

SUMMARY

Simple present

Mit dem *simple present* (einfache Gegenwart) sagst du, was jemand immer wieder oder gewohnheitsmäßig tut.

AUSSAGEN

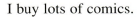

I buy lots of comics.

We sell toys.

She collects badges.

I play football. Ich spiele Fußball.
Tim and Pat read lots of books. Tim und Pat lesen viele Bücher.
Eric sells sweets every day. Eric verkauft jeden Tag Bonbons.
I have a cat. It plays in my room. Ich habe eine Katze. Sie spielt in meinem Zimmer.

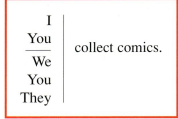

| I You We You They | collect comics. |

| He She It | eats fish. |

he, she, it
ein *s* muss mit!

Nach *he/she/it* hat das Verb eine *s*-Endung:
He eat**s** spaghetti.
She read**s** comics.

Pat (= She) play**s** tennis at school.
My friend (= He/She) buy**s** lots of computer games.

⚠ watch – watch**es**, go – go**es**

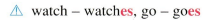

VERNEINUNGEN

I don't eat at *Burger World*. Ich esse nicht bei *Burger World*.
The shop doesn't sell cola. Der Laden verkauft keine Cola.
The pen doesn't write. Der Füller schreibt nicht.

Lass beim Verneinen nur ein *s* erscheinen!

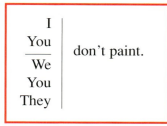

I	
You	
We	don't paint.
You	
They	

He	
She	doesn't paint.
It	

Die Langform von *don't* ist *do not*.

Die Langform von *doesn't* ist *does not*.

⚠ Mr Richardson sell**s** toys.
Mr Hill doe**s**n't sell toys.

this – that

This is my new CD.
Dies ist meine neue CD.

That's Mark's house, over there.
Das da drüben ist Marks Haus.

Du verwendest *this*, wenn etwas nahe ist. Wenn etwas weiter entfernt ist, verwendest du *that*.

IN DIESER UNIT HAST DU GELERNT,...

... zu sagen, was du oft tust.   ➡ *I read comics.*

... zu sagen, was du nicht tust.   ➡ *I don't play with trains.*

... zu sagen, was du magst oder nicht magst.   ➡ *I like dogs.*
I don't like cats.

... zu fragen, wie spät es ist.   ➡ *What time is it?*

... zu sagen, wie spät es ist.   ➡ *It's three fifteen.*

UNIT SIX
Weekends 🎧

A

In the week lots of people work.
Pupils go to school.
At the weekend people often have free time.
People often go to the shops.
Or they have jobs at home or in the garden.
They sometimes do their hobbies.
But some people work at the weekend, too.

And your weekends?
I do / don't have jobs at home.
I work / don't work in the garden.
I do / don't do a hobby.
My mum/dad works / doesn't work.
I like / don't like the weekends.

B Families at the weekends …

often

Families often go to the shops.
They often buy clothes or other things.
They often have jobs at home.
They often watch TV.

sometimes

Families sometimes visit places.
They sometimes go to the cinema.
They sometimes swim.
They sometimes visit friends.

Your family's weekends
We always …   We sometimes …
We often …   We never …

W 1-2

C

In England, four Mondays in spring and summer are holidays.
Lots of people don't work. They have long weekends.
The Kellys do different things at holiday weekends.

They visit interesting places.

Or they walk in the country.

Or they go to the zoo.

They visit the seaside.

They watch sports matches.

They go to fun parks.

D

Dave likes holiday weekends with his family.

DAVE	We often visit interesting places.
	Do you visit interesting places?
CLAIRE	No, we don't.
	Mum works at holiday weekends.
DAVE	Do you stay at home?
CLAIRE	Yes, we do.

EXERCISE 1 ■ Holiday weekends with the Kelly family

CLAIRE		DAVE
Do you	stay at home?	(✗) – No, we don't.
	walk in the country?	(✔) – Yes, we do.
	go to the cinema?	(✗) – No, …
	visit the seaside?	(✔) – Yes, …
	go to fun parks?	(✔) – …
	ride your bikes?	(✗) – …
	go to the shops?	(✗) – …

Holiday weekends in your family
Do you …?
– Yes, we do. We sometimes …
– No, we don't. We never …

✔ **CHECKPOINT**

Fragen über Gewohnheiten
Do you go to school? – Yes, I do.
Do they play tennis? – No, they don't.
Fragen mit *I/you/we/they* **fangen mit** *Do* **… an.**

W 3

EXERCISE 2 ■ What people like

DAVE I like holiday weekends.
Do you like holiday weekends, too?

CLAIRE I like cats.
Do you like …, too?

ADAM I … ice-cream.
Do you …, too?

ASIF I … comics.
Do …?

SHARON … dogs.
Do …?

EXERCISE 3 ■ What things do you like?

YOU
I like … Do you like …, too?

A PARTNER

dogs

hamburgers

comics

cats

bananas

games

…

 – Yes, I do. They're | great.
fun.
nice.

 – No, I don't. They aren't | interesting.
nice.

 – They're OK.

82

F

DAVE I have an idea for the holiday weekend.
Come to the country with us on Monday.
Visit my cousin.
She lives in the country.

CLAIRE Does your cousin live on a farm?

DAVE Yes, she does.

CLAIRE Does she have a brother or a sister?

DAVE No, she doesn't.
But she has two nice cousins!

EXERCISE 4 ■ Claire's other questions

1 Does your cousin live in a village?
2 Does your cousin go to school in a village?
3 … your uncle have a big farm?
4 … your aunt work on the farm?
5 … your cousin have an animal?
6 … your cousin like the country?

✔ **CHECKPOINT**

Fragen über Gewohnheiten
Does he work at home? – No, he doesn't.
Does she play tennis? – Yes, she does.
Fragen mit *he/she/it* fangen mit Does … an.

EXERCISE 5 ■ Now find Dave's answers to Claire's questions.

1 Does your cousin go to school in a village? – No, she doesn't.
She goes to school in a town.

2 Does your cousin live in a village? – …
3 … your uncle have a big farm? – …
4 … your aunt work on the farm?
5 … your cousin have an animal?
6 … your cousin like the country? W 4

– Yes, she does. She has a cat.

– No, she doesn't. My aunt works in a shop.

– No, she doesn't. But she lives near a village.

– No, she doesn't. She goes to school in a town.

– No, he doesn't. He has a small farm.

– Yes, she does. She likes the country.

STORY

On Monday Claire visited a farm with the Kellys.
It was her first day on a farm.

Rosedale Farm

"Your cousin Karen is lucky," Claire said. "She lives on a farm. Farms are great. Nice old houses, green fields, nice animals, ..."

"Oh, Claire!" Dave laughed. "Do you often go to the country?"

5 "No, I don't," Claire said. "But there are always lots of animals on farms. I want to take photos of them. Does the farm have cows?"

"No, it doesn't," Dave said.

"Does it have chickens?"

10 "No, it doesn't."

"Do they have pigs and sheep on the farm?"

"No, they don't," Dave said.

"Do they have other animals?"

"They have a cat."

"The farm has cereals, Claire,"   15
Mrs Kelly said, "and some potatoes, too."

"Oh. Well, I want to ride on the tractor," Claire said.

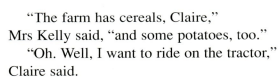

Rosedale Farm was a surprise for Claire. It was OK. But the house was very modern. 20 Claire was sad. The farm had no animals. Dave's uncle was very busy – but not with the tractor. He was at the computer. Karen's mother had some nice cakes on the table in the living-room. 25

84

"Do you like our farm, Claire?" Karen asked.

"It's OK. But you don't have animals. "

"Our neighbours have chickens," Karen said. That was interesting for Dave.

"That's nice. Do you often visit their farm? Let's feed their chickens," he said.

30 "But they have hundreds of chickens!" Karen said. "Modern farms are different from the farms in books."

Karen's mother had an idea. "Listen. There's a place with lots of farm animals. Families with children often go 35 there. They have cows and sheep, and an old tractor, too."

"Great!" Dave and Claire said. "Is it far?"

"No, it isn't. It's very near."

40 "Where is it, Mum?" Karen asked.

"It's the farm museum near York. Let's go in the car."

"OK. Let's go to a town and visit a farm!" Claire laughed.

Some modern farms don't have animals. But at farm museums there are lots of animals and other interesting things, too.

TASK A ■ What? Who? Where?
1 What was the farm's name?
2 Who was sad?
3 Who was very busy?
4 Where was Dave's uncle?
5 What was at the other farm?
6 Where was the museum?

TASK B ■■ In the story find …
1 … five animals.
2 … three people in families.
3 … the opposite of: new, town, never, far.
4 … the plural of: house, sheep, potato, family, child, museum.

W 5-6

ACTIVE ENGLISH

ACTIONS 🎧 Über Freizeit und Hobbys sprechen

Was für ein Hobby hat Tim?

TIM Do you play sport in your free time?

ALAN I play tennis.

TIM I don't play sport.

ALAN What's your hobby?

TIM I make models of cars.

EXERCISE 1 ■ **People do different things in their free time.**

1 People sometimes take photos.
2 People sometimes play computer games.
3 People sometimes play …
4 People sometimes listen to …
5 People sometimes …
6 People …

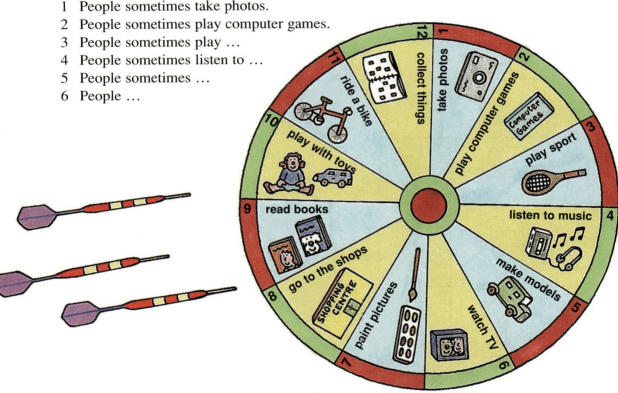

EXERCISE 2 ■ **What about your free time?**

YOU	A PARTNER
1 Do you take photos?	– Yes, I do.
2 Do you play …?	– No, I don't.

W 7

Was macht Tina gern in ihrer Freizeit?

ALISON I like skateboarding.
I'm good at skateboarding.

TINA I like computer games and swimming.
I'm not good at skateboarding.

EXERCISE 3 ■ **Pat's hobbies**

Pat likes skating.

She likes football.

… painting.

… computer games.

… swimming.

… reading. W 8

Do you like Pat's hobbies?
I like …   I'm good at …
I don't like … I'm not good at …

ACTIVITY Our free time

Make a poster about your class.

11 pupils play football
8 pupils read comics
5 pupils listen to music
3 pupils play computer games
2 pupils paint pictures

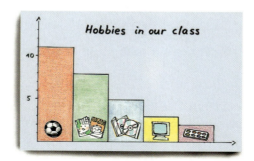

Hobbies in our class

LOOK AROUND YOU Sport

Some sports have English names
in German. What are the names of
the sports in the pictures?

Baseball ▪ Basketball ▪ Golf
Hockey ▪ Jogging ▪ Tennis

1

2

3

4

5

6

PRACTICE PAGES

STRUCTURES

EXERCISE 1 ■ Pocket-money

Dave		Sharon
sometimes	**magazines**	often
often	**snacks**	never
never	**games**	sometimes
never	**clothes**	often
sometimes	**computer games**	never
sometimes	**sweets**	sometimes
never	**CDs**	often

Dave sometimes buys magazines.
He often buys snacks.
He never buys games.
He never buys …
He sometimes buys …
He …

Sharon often buys …
She never …
She …

> **And your pocket-money?**
>
> I | sometimes
> | often | buy …
> | never

EXERCISE 2 ■ There's a new pupil at Brookland School.

Do ▪ Does

1 … you come from Chester?
2 … you have a brother or a sister?
3 … your brother go to this school?
4 … he work in Chester?
5 … your sisters have jobs?
6 … they go to school?
7 … your house have a big garden?
8 … you like Chester?

EXERCISE 3 ■■ Pat wants to buy a walkman. Make her questions with *Do/Does*.

1 *Do you sell* walkmans? – Yes, we sell walkmans.
2 … *have* a cheap walkman? – Yes, we have a very cheap walkman.
3 … a radio? – No, it doesn't have a radio.
4 … £30? – No, it doesn't. It costs £19.99.
5 … batteries? – Yes, we sell *Star* batteries. £5.40 for six.
6 … cheaper batteries? – No, we don't. We only sell *Star* batteries.

W 9-10

SITUATIONS

Wie sagst du auf Englisch, dass …

1 … du Wochenenden magst?
2 … du eine Idee hast?
3 … etwas ganz in der Nähe ist?
4 … du keinen Sport treibst?

Wie fragst du auf Englisch, …

5 … ob jemand zur Schule geht?
6 … ob jemand oft aufs Land fährt?
7 … ob etwas weit ist?
8 … welches Hobby jemand hat?

Tip: Look again at pages 80-87.

WORDPOWER

WORDPOWER 1 ■ **Make the 20 words.**

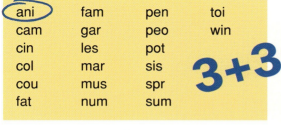

ani	fam	pen	toi
cam	gar	peo	win
cin	les	pot	
col	mar	sis	
cou	mus	spr	
fat	num	sum	

3+3=6

	cil	her	mer
	den	ily	our
	dow	ing	ple
	ema	ket	sin
ato	era	let	son
ber	eum	mal	ter

ani + mal = animal

WORDPOWER 2 ■ **Actions: Find the right word.**

b u y ▪ c o l l e c t ▪ e a t ▪ l i k e ▪ l i s t e n ▪ l o o k ▪ m e e t ▪

w o r k ▪ w r i t e

p a i n t ▪ p l a y

▪ w a s h   u p ▪ w a l k ▪ t h r o w ▪ s w i m ▪ s i t ▪ r i d e ▪ r e a d ▪

W 11

SOUNDS 🎧

[f]: for, fun, after, enough, laugh
[v]: very, above, evening, have, live
[w]: watch, weekend, what, swim, walk

[f] - [v] - [w]: village, window, five,
one, white, sweets, leave, work

SPECIAL TOPIC

My weekdays

LIZ Every weekday – Monday, Tuesday, Wednesday, Thursday, Friday – I go to school.

I get up at 7.30.

I have a wash.

I have breakfast.

I clean my teeth.

I leave the house at 8.30.

At 6.00 I have my evening meal.

I go to bed at 9.30 …

… and count the days till Saturday and Sunday – the weekend!

EXERCISE ■ Their weekdays

Dave and Adam

They get up at 7.15.
They have breakfast at …
They go to school at …
They come … at …
In the evenings they …

They … at …

	Dave and Adam	Sharon
get up	7.15	7.30
have breakfast	7.45	8.00
go to school	8.35	8.30
come home	4.20	4.15
In the evenings?	watch TV or read comics	watches TV
go to bed	9.45	9.30

Sharon

She gets up at …
She has … at …
She goes … at …
She comes … at …
In the evenings she …

She … at …

And your weekdays? I get up at …

W 12-13

90

SONG 🎧 Five days a week and all the year

Verse 1

When I get up at eight,
I feel very slow,
I go to the bathroom,
Oh no, no, no, no!
I do it every morning,
Five days a week
    and all the year.

Verse 2

Then I have a quick wash,
I put on my things,
I go to the kitchen,
Where the radio sings.
I do it every morning,
Five days a week
    and all the year.

Verse 3

Then I eat up my toast,
I don't talk very much,
I leave our house,
And I run for the bus.
I do it every morning,
Five days a week
    and all the year.

Verse 4

At the end of the day,
It's my bedtime at ten,
A few hours later,
It all starts again.
I do it every morning,
Five days a week
    and all the year.

LISTENING 🎧 With the animals

1 Where are the children? Listen.

At a farm museum. ▪ At a farm near Chester. ▪ At Rosedale Farm.

2 Listen again. Make the story with the four pictures.

1 Picture …   2 Picture …   3 Picture …   4 Picture …

Picture a

Picture b

Picture c

Picture d

W 14-15

91

SUMMARY

Simple present

Mit dem *simple present* (einfache Gegenwart) sagst du, was jemand immer (wieder) tut.

Ann eats hamburgers.	I swim every day.	We often buy CDs.
Ann isst Hamburger.	Ich schwimme jeden Tag.	Wir kaufen oft CDs.

Häufig stehen bei dieser Form auch Wörter oder Ausdrücke, die sagen, wie oft etwas geschieht.

every day jeden Tag	**always** immer
every week jede Woche	**often** oft
on Tuesday dienstags	**sometimes** manchmal
at the weekend am Wochenende	**never** nie

WORTSTELLUNG

⚠ Beachte die Wortstellung bei *always, often, sometimes, never.*

We always buy cola.	Luke sometimes reads.	I never eat fish.
Wir kaufen immer Cola.	Luke liest manchmal.	Ich esse nie Fisch.

FRAGEN

Fragen in der einfachen Gegenwart stellst du mit *Do* oder *Does.*

Bei *I/you/we/they* bildest du Fragen mit *Do.* Bei *he/she/it* bildest du Fragen mit *Does.*

Do	I you we you they	paint good pictures?

Does	he she it	live in a big house?

⚠ Auch bei *have* bildest du Fragen mit *Do/Does*:

I have a dog. **Do** you **have** a dog?
Do they have a flat?
Does Pat **have** the money?
Does your brother have a bike?

⚠ Debbie like**s** cats.
Doe**s** Debbie like dogs?

Nur ein *s* – in Fragen bei *doe**s***!

KURZANTWORTEN

Fragen mit *Do*/*Does* werden häufig mit Kurzantworten – nicht nur mit *Yes* oder *No* – beantwortet.

> Do you play tennis? – Yes, I do.
> – No, I don't.

> Does Pat live here? – Yes, she does.
> – No, she doesn't.

Do you like our bike? – Yes, I do.
Do you have a bike? – No, I don't.

IN DIESER UNIT HAST DU GELERNT,...

... zu sagen, wie oft jemand etwas tut.	➡ *I often play football.* *We sometimes ride our bikes.*
... zu fragen, was jemand gewöhnlich tut.	➡ *Do you work in a shop?* *Does your brother go to school?*
... zu fragen, ob jemand etwas besitzt.	➡ *Does your cousin have an animal?* *Do you have a walkman?*
... zu fragen, ob jemand etwas mag.	➡ *Do you like animals?*
... über deine Hobbys zu sprechen.	➡ *I play tennis.*

DU KANNST AUCH VERSTEHEN, WIE ...

... jemand sagt, was er/sie gern tut.	➡ *I like swimming.*
... jemand sagt, ob er/sie etwas gut/ nicht gut kann.	➡ *I'm good at tennis.* *I'm not good at swimming.*
... über die Vergangenheit berichtet wird.	➡ *Tom visited a farm.* *"I want to ride on the tractor," he said.*

UNIT SEVEN
Our town 🎧

A Here are some places in a town centre. Where can you go in a town?

You can go to the supermarket.

You can go to the cinema.

You can go to the market.

You can go to the library.

You can go to the pet shop.

You can go to the sports centre.

> **Where can you go in your town?**
> We can go to the hamburger restaurant.
> We can go to the shops. We can go to …

W 1

EXERCISE 1 ■ What can you do in a town?

1 You can … things at the shops.
2 You can … a meal at a restaurant.
3 You can … films at the cinema.
4 You can … new computer games.
5 You can … at the sports centre.

6 You can … friends.
7 You can … new CDs.
8 You can … to the library.

buy ▪ eat ▪ go ▪ listen to ▪ meet
play ▪ swim ▪ watch

We can watch good films at …
We can swim at …

We can eat good meals at …
We can buy good CDs at …

W 2

B

And Sundays in Chester? Where can you go on Sundays?

You can go to the big shops.

… to the cinema.

… to the sports centre.

But some places in Chester town centre aren't open on Sundays.

You can't go to the small shops.

You can't go to the library.

You can't go to the pet shop.

EXERCISE 2 ■ Sundays in Chester town centre

1 (big shops ✔ market ✘) People can go to the big shops. But they can't go to the market.
2 (sports centre ✔ library ✘) They can go to the … But they can't …
3 (cinema ✔ pet shop ✘) They can … But they can't …
4 (supermarket ✔ small shops ✘) They … But they …

Sunday in your town
We can go to the …
We can't go to the …

C Asif is in the kitchen with his mother.

> **ASIF** Can I go to Dave's house, Mum?
>
> **MRS AHMED** Yes, you can. OK.
>
> **ASIF** Can we go to town, too?
>
> **MRS AHMED** No, you can't. Sorry.
> You boys are too young.
>
> **ASIF** Oh, Mum. Please.
>
> **MRS AHMED** Come with dad and me on Saturday.
> We want wallpaper, curtains
> and cushions.
>
> **ASIF** It isn't fun in town with you and dad.

EXERCISE 3 ■ Make other dialogues.

ASIF	MRS AHMED
Can I go to Dave's house?	Yes, you can. OK.
Can I go to town?	No, you can't. Sorry.

✔ Dave's house
✘ town

✔ Claire's house
✘ the football match

✔ the cinema
✘ the shops

✔ the library
✘ the market

✔ the pet shop
✘ the sports centre

YOU	A PARTNER
Can you watch TV in the mornings?	– Yes, I can.
Can you ride your bike to school?	– No, I can't.
Can you go to bed late at the weekend?	
Can you go to town with your friends?	
Can you ride your bike to town?	
Can you play football in the kitchen?	
Can you make snacks for your friends?	

W 3-4

D On Friday evening the Ahmeds are very busy. They're working in the living-room.

E

MR AHMED	Next week the room will have new wallpaper.
	It'll have new curtains.
	And we'll have new cushions.
	The living-room will be very nice.
MRS AHMED	Asif will come to town with us tomorrow.
	He'll help us.

EXERCISE 4 ■ But Asif has other ideas.

1	Chester		in the shops.
2	Our shop		terrible.
3	The car parks	will be	on TV!
4	Lots of people		full of cars.
5	Manchester United		very busy.

ASIF	1 Chester will be terrible.
	2 Our shop will be … W 5

✔ CHECKPOINT

Was sein wird:
The letter <mark>will be</mark> here tomorrow.
Chester City <mark>will play</mark> on Sunday.

F

MRS AHMED	We can go to town in the morning.
	We can park near the market. I'm sure it'll be OK.
ASIF	But can we go to *Chester Sports*, too?
	Chester Sports has the new Manchester United shirts.
MR AHMED	They'll be very expensive.
	And we won't have time.
	But we can buy some new jeans for you.
ASIF	*TeenScene* is a good shop for jeans.
MR AHMED	*TeenScene!* Will jeans be expensive there?
	You aren't careful with money, Asif. The market is the cheapest.

G

Asif is in town with his mother and father. They're in the market hall.

STORY

Mr Ahmed is careful with money – but not always.

Come on, Asif!

Asif was in the market hall with his parents. He had a big bag of cushions.
He was at a very good sweet stall.

MR AHMED	Come on, Asif. There are sweets in our shop.
ASIF	OK, OK. Let's go to *Chester Sports*.
5	They have some great football shirts.
MRS AHMED	We can't go there with all our bags!
ASIF	Oh Mum, it isn't far from here.
MRS AHMED	Sports shops are expensive, Asif.
MR AHMED	And the market is cheaper. It'll have good
10	clothes. Let's buy Asif's jeans now.
ASIF	Jeans from the market? Ugh!
	Let's go to *TeenScene* in Lee Road.
MR AHMED	Come on, Asif. Sweets, football shirts,
	expensive jeans.
15	You aren't careful enough with money.

At a clothes stall they looked at the jeans.
Asif liked the red jeans. Red was his favourite colour.
But Mr Ahmed said no. Black was the nicest colour.
Asif was sad. His parents had no idea!

But ten minutes later they had the jeans – 20
black again.
Mr Ahmed had the money in his wallet.
Asif was next to his father with the cush-
ions.
Mrs Ahmed looked at a clock. It was late. 25
And their car was in the car park.
They only had eight minutes.

It was later now. They only had five minutes.

MRS AHMED	Come on, Asif. We'll be late.
ASIF	I'm coming – with all the cushions.
MR AHMED	Oh no!
ASIF	What's the matter, Dad?
MR AHMED	Where's my wallet – with my money and my credit cards?
ASIF	Is this your wallet, Dad?
MR AHMED	Yes, it is. But where …?
ASIF	At the clothes stall.
MR AHMED	Oh, yes …! Thank you, Asif.
ASIF	I *can* sometimes be careful with money.
MR AHMED	OK, OK. Come on, Asif. Let's go to the car. Then we can go to *Chester Sports* and buy that football shirt.
ASIF	Great!

30, 35, 40 *(line numbers)*

A football shirt from Asif's favourite team

TASK A ■ **What's wrong?**
1 The Ahmeds are at *TeenScene*.
  – *The Ahmeds are in the market hall.*
2 *Chester Sports* is cheap.
3 Asif's jeans are from a sweet stall.
4 Blue is Asif's favourite colour.
5 There are some credit cards in Mr Ahmed's bag.
6 Asif can have a football bag.

TASK B ■■ **Was it Asif, Mrs Ahmed or Mr Ahmed?**
1 "There are sweets in our shop."
2 "Can I have a new football shirt?"
3 "This big bag of cushions is terrible."
4 "The red jeans are the nicest."
5 "We'll be late at the car park."
6 "OK. We can buy a football shirt."

W 6-7

ACTIVE ENGLISH

ACTIONS 🎧 Über Wünsche sprechen

Wie viele Cassetten kauft Tom?

BOY Hallo. What would you like?

TOM I'd like two C90 cassettes, please.

BOY Three cassettes are cheaper. Look.

TOM OK. I'd like three then.

BOY Here you are. Anything else?

TOM No, thank you.

Was kauft Jenny?

JENNY I'd like a red T-shirt, please.

WOMAN What size? Small?

JENNY Yes, please.

WOMAN Sorry. There isn't a small T-shirt in red. Only blue or white.

JENNY OK. I'd like a blue T-shirt.

EXERCISE 1 ■ What would you like?

1 I'd like a bag, please.   2 I'd like …

  1   2   3   4   5   6

EXERCISE 2 ■ In shops: Make the dialogues.

1 Can I have a *Chox*, please?

2 Jeans? What size?

3 How much is the *Naido* walkman?

4 Would you like the red or the blue pen?

5 Can I help you?

6 I'd like the new *Kids* CD, please.

- I'm not sure. Size 26 or 28.
- Here you are. 30 p, please.
- Can I have four *AA* batteries, please?
- I'd like the red pen, please.
- They're next to the door.
- It's only £29.90.

W 8

EXERCISE 3 ■ **In a shop: Make a dialogue with a partner.**

Frage, was die Kundin / der Kunde möchte.	▶	Sage, dass du ein *Kids* Poster möchtest.
Sage, dass du zwei Poster hast.	▶	Frage, wie viel das kleine Poster kostet.
Sage, dass es £5 kostet.	▶	Sage, dass du das kleine Poster möchtest.
Frage, ob sonst noch etwas gebraucht wird.	▶	Sage nein. Bedanke dich.

W 9

GAME Let's go to the shops and buy …

Make a chain.

Let's go to the shops.

Let's go to the shops *and buy a comic.*

Let's go to the shops and buy a comic *and a CD.*

Let's go to the shops and buy a comic, a CD *and a football.*

Let's go to the shops and buy a comic, a CD, a …

LOOK AROUND YOU Clothes

There are English and American words for clothes in Germany.

What's the right word?

1   2   3   4

5   6   7

Anorak
Baseballcap ▪ Jeans
Pullover ▪ Shorts
Sweatshirt ▪ T-Shirt

PRACTICE PAGES

STRUCTURES

EXERCISE 1 ■ Not here!

eat ▪ park ▪ play ▪ ride ▪ run ▪ work

1 You can't work here!

2 You can't … here!

3 You can't …

4 …

5 …

6 …

EXERCISE 2 ■ Pupilmatic – a great idea. What will it do for pupils? Find six things.

1 It'll write maths exercises.
2 It'll …
3 It'll …
4 …   5 …   6 …

It'll	write	sweets for you.
	make	after meals.
	buy	hamburgers.
	wash up	to school for you.
	play	maths exercises.
	go	football with you.

EXERCISE 3 ■ At school or in a shop?

1 Let's read a story. – *At school.*
2 I'd like the red pullover.
3 What size is it?
4 You'll watch a video tomorrow.
5 Will *Pop* magazine come next week?
6 What's *Tante* in English?
7 Write exercise 4, please.
8 That's £10, please.
9 Can I read, please?
10 Hallo. What would you like?

EXERCISE 4 ■■ Can you make the shop dialogue with the woman and the girl?

"Oh! No, thank you. I'm sure other shops will have them."
"Here you are. *Longer Life* batteries are very good."
"But there are six batteries here."
"Yes, please. I'd like two AA batteries."
"Hallo. Can I help you?"
"That's right. Will six be OK?"   W 10-11

Can you write a shop dialogue, too?

102

SITUATIONS

Wie sagst du auf Englisch, dass …
1 … etwas keinen Spaß macht?
2 … du dich langweilst?
3 … ihr euch verspäten werdet?

Wie fragst du jemanden auf Englisch, …
4 … wohin man sonntags gehen kann?
5 … ob du in die Stadt gehen darfst?
6 … was er/sie gerne hätte?

Tip: Look again at pages 94-100.

WORDPOWER

WORDPOWER 1 ■ Places, people, time   Vorsicht! Beachte die Großschreibung bei Eigennamen!

Where?	heretherechesterenglandeuropeinabovebrooklandschooltown

Who?	youmrskellytheyclairegirldaveteacherterrysisterwetomboys

When?	nowsummermondaydayafternoontuesdayalwaysmonthspring

WORDPOWER 2 ■ Make a new, longer word.

1 bed…
2 super…
3 post…

4 foot…
5 week…
6 cheese…

WORDPOWER 3 ■ What's the wrong word in the group?

1 mother ▪ computer ▪ neighbour ▪ teacher ▪ woman
2 library ▪ supermarket ▪ money ▪ pet shop ▪ market ▪ cinema
3 curtain ▪ book ▪ wallpaper ▪ cushion ▪ table ▪ chair
4 pullover ▪ jeans ▪ shirt ▪ wallet ▪ T-shirt
5 nice ▪ great ▪ OK ▪ good ▪ super ▪ bored
6 far ▪ go ▪ leave ▪ ride ▪ walk ▪ run ▪ swim   W 12

SOUNDS 🎧

[ɑː]: car, bathroom, park, class, card, far
[æ]: man, flat, bag, cat, and, match
[e]: men, pen, ten, next, red, bed, when

[ɑː] - [æ] - [e]: man - men, badge - bed,
apple - Elm, Pat - park, animal - aunt,
cat - car

SPECIAL TOPIC

The year

There are twelve months in the year.

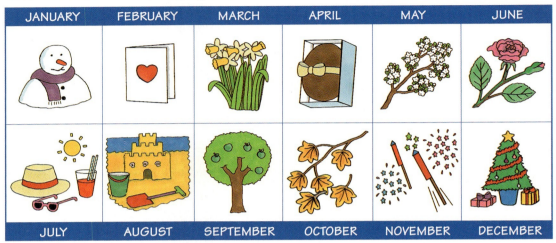

There are some special days in Britain and the USA.

New Year's Day

Thanksgiving Day (USA)

Christmas Day

Independence Day (USA)

Halloween

Guy Fawkes Night (Britain)

New Year's Day is in January.
Thanksgiving Day is in …
Christmas Day is in … W 13

There are four seasons in the year.

spring   **summer**   **autumn**   **winter**

EXERCISE ■ **The seasons**

1   What months are in spring?
2   What months are in summer?

3   What months are in autumn?
4   What months are in winter?   W 14

SONG **Calendar calypso**

January, February, March,
April, May, June, July.
August, September,
October, November, December.

LISTENING **On Saturday**

1   **What programme is it? Listen.**

A children's radio programme. ▪ A children's TV programme. ▪ A film about Saturday.

2   **What's wrong with the posters? Listen again.**

1 It isn't on …
  It's on …

2 It isn't at …
  It's at …

3 It isn't a …
  It's a …

4 It isn't a …
  It's …

5 It isn't in …
  It's …

W 15-16

SUMMARY

can

Mit *can* sagt man, was jemand tun kann oder tun darf.

Mary can ride a bike.

Can you help me, please?

Sue can't have a cake.

AUSSAGEN

I/You/He/She/It We/You/They	can make cakes.

I can play tennis.
Ich kann Tennis spielen.

VERNEINUNGEN

I/You/He/She/It We/You/They	can't make ice-cream.

Kevin Payne can't write.
Kevin Payne kann nicht schreiben.

Die Langform von *can't* ist *cannot*.

FRAGEN UND KURZANTWORTEN

Can	I/you/he/she/it we/you/they	make ice-cream?

Can I go to Tim's house?
Kann/Darf ich zu Tim gehen?

Can I go to the shops? – Yes, you can.
Can Tim come with me? – No, he can't.
Can Claire ride a bike? – Yes, she can.
Can you ride a bike? – No, I can't.

What can we do? – We can play football.
Where can we play? – In the field.
When can we go there? – At 3 o'clock.

will

Mit dem *will-future* sagst du, was in der Zukunft geschehen wird (z.B. bei Vorhersagen und Vermutungen).

The film tomorrow will be very good.
Der Film morgen wird sehr gut sein.
I'm sure we'll be late.
Ich bin sicher, wir werden zu spät kommen.

AUSSAGEN

I/You/He/She/It We/You/They	will be at home tomorrow.

Tomorrow will be a very nice day.

Die Kurzform von *will* ist *'ll* : *I'll* ▪ *You'll* ▪ *He'll* ▪ *She'll* ▪ *It'll* ▪ *We'll* ▪ *You'll* ▪ *They'll*
Mit *won't* (= will not) wird gesagt, was voraussichtlich nicht sein wird.
The new *Kids* CD won't be cheap.   Die neue *Kids* CD wird nicht billig sein.

IN DIESER UNIT HAST DU GELERNT,...

... zu sagen, dass du etwas kannst/darfst. ➡ *I can swim.*
I can go to Tim's party.

... über Dinge in der Zukunft zu sprechen. ➡ *It'll be a nice day tomorrow.*

... zu sagen, dass du etwas möchtest. ➡ *I'd like the red pullover.*

... über das Jahr zu sprechen. ➡ *Christmas is in December.*

DU KANNST AUCH VERSTEHEN, WIE ...

... Dinge miteinander verglichen werden. ➡ *The red bike is nice.*
The blue bike is nicer.
The green bike is the nicest.

... gesagt wird, was in der Zukunft nicht geschehen wird. ➡ *The sports shop won't be open.*

... Fragen über die Zukunft gestellt werden. ➡ *Will the shop be open tomorrow?*

Christmas and New Year are holidays in Britain and America, too.

Merry Christmas! Happy New Year!

Here are some British Christmas things.

Christmas food

Christmas cards

Presents on Christmas Day

Dear Santa,
I am a very good boy.
Please put a walkman and
some new comics in my
stocking this Christmas.
Thank you very much.
Lots of love
Michael xx

A letter to Father Christmas

Father Christmas

Christmas crackers (with a present, a joke and a hat)

ACTIVITY Christmas cards

Make an English Christmas card.

- Happy Christmas
- Merry Christmas
- Happy New Year
- Best wishes for Christmas and the New Year
- With love from ….

SONG We wish you a merry Christmas

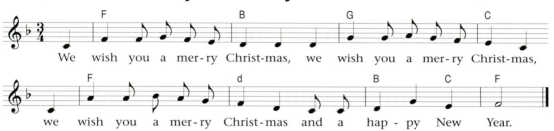

We wish you a mer-ry Christ-mas, we wish you a mer-ry Christ-mas,

we wish you a mer-ry Christ-mas and a hap-py New Year.

Glad tidings we bring,
To you and your kin.
We wish you a merry Christmas
And a happy New Year.

*EXTRA PAGES 2 🎧

Four friends, three bikes, two boxes ... and one puncture!

Bikes and boxes

What are your ideas for the weekend?

Let's ride our bikes to Woodlake.

Good idea. Let's have a picnic. It's nice there.

WOODLAKE 10 MILES

It's a long journey to Woodlake.

And my old bike isn't very good.

Oh, Sharon. Please come.

I have an idea. There's a bus from Chester. Let's meet at Woodlake.

Let's make sandwiches for the picnic. My sandwiches are good.

We have drinks in our shop.

I can take the sandwiches and drinks.

I have some tools for the bike journey.

OK. Let's meet at Dave's house on Saturday.

It's Saturday morning.

On the bike journey …

Sharon is at Woodlake.

TASK A ■ Right or wrong?

1 Woodlake is in Chester.
2 Sharon has a new bike.
3 There's a bus to Woodlake.
4 Dave's sandwiches are good.
5 Asif has the drinks.
6 Sharon has a puncture.
7 Asif, Claire and Dave have the tools.
8 Sharon has the sandwiches.

TASK B ■ ■ On the bike journey

Claire ▪ eat ▪ picnic ▪ sandwich
tools ▪ Woodlake

ASIF A puncture! What now?

DAVE Your bike is good, …
Ride to … and bring the …

CLAIRE OK. But I'm hungry.
Dave, a …, please!

ASIF No. Let's … with Sharon.

DAVE Yes, let's have the … in Woodlake.

*EXTRA PAGES 3 🎧

A big problem for Claire. She was without her bike.

Where's my bike?

It was Sunday morning. Mrs Hall had no tea.
So Claire went to the *8 till late* shop.
She went on her bike, of course.
She liked her red *Speed* bike.

1

5 Claire was in front of the shop. She had the tea.
But where was her bike? Was this Asif's and
Dave's joke?
Claire looked behind the shop.
There was no bike in front of the shop, and
10 no bike behind the shop.
And new bikes were very expensive – too
expensive for Claire's mum.

2

It was after school on Monday.
Mrs Hall went to the police station with Claire.
15 They looked at the bikes – old bikes, new
bikes, big bikes and small bikes.
But Claire didn't see her bike there.

3

There was a poster at the police station.
It was about bike auctions.
20 But the next auction was in October.
   "I'm sorry, Claire. Now you're without
a bike for the summer," Mrs Hall said.
Claire was very sad.

4

Three months later Mrs Hall and Claire went to the police auction. Perhaps there was a bike for
25 Claire. But Mrs Hall didn't have enough money for a good bike.

5

"Let's go home, Claire," she said. "My £60 isn't enough. But it'll be Christmas soon."
30 "Christmas! Christmas is months from now," Claire said.

Claire and her mum went to the door. Then the man said,
"Here's the next bike. Number 97.
35 A red *Speed* bike. £20? £25? …"
Claire and Mrs Hall went back.
It was Claire's bike!

6

"My bike! After three months! Great! Can I ride it home, Mum?"
Mrs Hall laughed.
40 "First we can go to a bike shop.
They'll have a good early Christmas present for you – a bike lock!"

TASK A ■ **What? When? Where? Who?**
1 Who had no tea?
2 What wasn't behind the shop?
3 Where was the poster?
4 When was the next auction?
5 What was number 97?
6 What will Claire's early Christmas present be?

TASK B ■■ **A bike for the summer**

had ▪ looked ▪ laughed
said ▪ was

In the summer, Claire … no bike.
But her mum's big, old bike … in the garage. Dave and Asif … at it.
"You can't ride that," Asif …
But Claire only …

Vocabulary

Dieses Wörterverzeichnis enthält alle neuen Wörter des Buches in der Reihenfolge, in der sie im Buch zum ersten Mal vorkommen.

Der Pfeil bedeutet: Schau in die rechte Spalte.

Hier sind Wörter in Gruppen zusammengefasst. Das macht das Lernen leichter.

Diese Zahl gibt die Seite an, auf der die Wörter zum ersten Mal vorkommen.

Die ganz schwarz gedruckten Wörter sind besonders wichtig.

Schräg gestellte Wörter kommen in Spielen, Liedern, Reimen usw. vor.

Normal gedruckte Wörter sind wichtig für das Kapitel, in dem sie vorkommen.

In diesem Abschnitt kannst du selbst überprüfen, ob du Wörter richtig verstanden hast.

Dieses Zeichen bedeutet „Aufgepasst!".

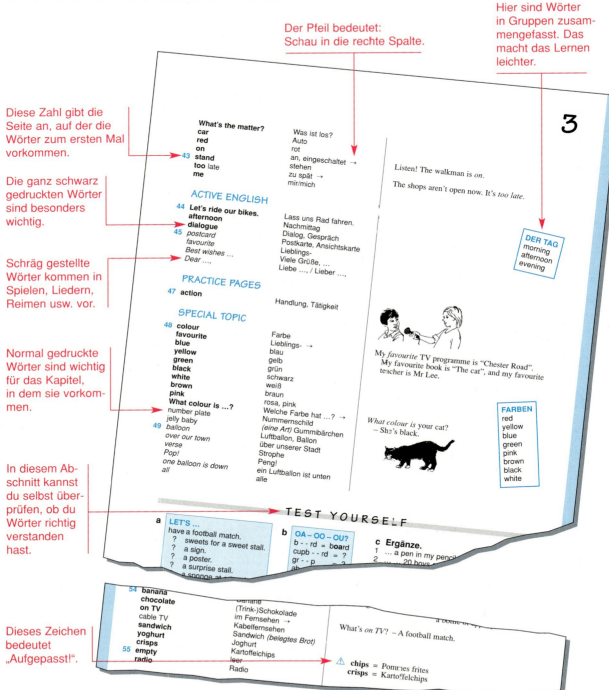

3

	What's the matter?	Was ist los?
	car	Auto
	red	rot
	on	an, eingeschaltet →
43	stand	stehen
	too late	zu spät →
	me	mir/mich

Listen! The walkman is *on*.

The shops aren't open now. It's *too late*.

ACTIVE ENGLISH

44	**Let's ride our bikes.**	Lass uns Rad fahren.
	afternoon	Nachmittag
	dialogue	Dialog, Gespräch
45	postcard	Postkarte, Ansichtskarte
	favourite	Lieblings-
	Best wishes …	Viele Grüße, …
	Dear …,	Liebe …, / Lieber …,

DER TAG
morning
afternoon
evening

PRACTICE PAGES

47	action	Handlung, Tätigkeit

SPECIAL TOPIC

48	**colour**	Farbe
	favourite	Lieblings- →
	blue	blau
	yellow	gelb
	green	grün
	black	schwarz
	white	weiß
	brown	braun
	pink	rosa, pink
	What colour is …?	Welche Farbe hat …? →
	number plate	Nummernschild
	jelly baby	(eine Art) Gummibärchen
49	balloon	Luftballon, Ballon
	over our town	über unserer Stadt
	verse	Strophe
	Pop!	Peng!
	one balloon is down	ein Luftballon ist unten
	all	alle

My *favourite* TV programme is "Chester Road". My favourite book is "The cat", and my favourite teacher is Mr Lee.

What colour is your cat? – She's black.

FARBEN
red
yellow
blue
green
pink
brown
black
white

TEST YOURSELF

a **LET'S …**
have a football match.
? sweets for a sweet stall.
? a sign.
? a poster.
? a surprise stall.
a sponge at …

b **OA – OO – OU?**
b - - rd = **board**
cupb - - rd = ?
gr - - p = ?
ab … = ?

c **Ergänze.**
1 … a pen in my pencil …
2 … 20 boys …

54	**banana**	Banane
	chocolate	(Trink-)Schokolade
	on TV	im Fernsehen →
	cable TV	Kabelfernsehen
	sandwich	Sandwich (belegtes Brot)
	yoghurt	Joghurt
	crisps	Kartoffelchips
55	**empty**	leer
	radio	Radio

a bottle of …

What's *on TV*? – A football match.

⚠ **chips** = Pommes frites
crisps = Kartoffelchips

START HERE ... VOCABULARY

6	Start here ...	Fang hier an ... / Fangt hier an ...
	Germany	Deutschland
	is	ist
	in	in
	Europe	Europa
	too	auch →
	a	ein/eine
	town	Stadt →
7	**I'm (= I am)**	ich bin →
	from	von; aus →
	here's (= here is)	hier ist
	my	mein/meine
	house	Haus
	number	Nummer; Zahl; Ziffer
	flat	Wohnung
	above	über
	shop	Laden, Geschäft
	new	neu
8	**or**	oder
	I'm at school.	Ich bin in der Schule; Ich gehe zur Schule. →
	and	und →
	you	du; ihr; Sie →
9	*Start again ...*	Fang/Fangt noch einmal (von vorn) an ...
	name card	Namensschild
	for your English lesson	für deinen/euren Englisch-unterricht
	name	Name
	Look here.	Schau/Schaut (hier)her.
	please	bitte
	Listen.	Hör zu. / Hört zu.
	Write ...	Schreib ... / Schreibt ...
	exercise	Übung
	Open your books.	Schlagt eure Bücher auf.

Dresden is in Germany. Augsburg is in Germany, *too*.

Passau is a *town* in Germany.

I'm from Stuttgart. – I'm from Dortmund.

I'm at school.

I'm at Erich-Kästner-Schule. *And you?*
– I'm at Erich-Kästner-Schule, too.

TEST YOURSELF

a GEBÄUDE

school   ?   ?

b Ergänze.
1 Chester is in England. London is in England, ...
2 Potsdam is a ... in Germany.
3 ...'m from Bamberg.
4 I'm ... school.
5 I'm at Süd-Schule. And ...? – I'm at Süd-Schule, too .

UNIT ONE VOCABULARY

10	**Hallo.**	Hallo. Guten Tag.
	road	Straße
	What's your name?	Wie heißt du? / Wie heißen Sie? (Wie ist dein/Ihr Name?) →
	Where are you from?	Wo kommst du her? →
	How old are you?	Wie alt bist du? →
11	**what's (= what is)**	was ist
	your	dein/deine; euer/eure; Ihr/Ihre →
	badge	Abzeichen; Button →
	yes	ja
	stupid	dumm, blöd
	no	nein
	not	nicht →
	you're (= you are)	du bist; ihr seid; Sie sind
	very	sehr
	unfriendly	unfreundlich →
	terrible	schrecklich, fürchterlich
	football team	Fußballmannschaft →
12	**they're (= they are)**	sie sind
	Mrs	Frau *(vor Namen)*
	boy, boys	Junge, Jungen →
	nice	nett; schön →
	but	aber
	big	groß
	perhaps	vielleicht
	different	andere/anderer/anderes; verschieden, anders
	class, classes	Klasse, Klassen
13	**Good morning.**	Guten Morgen.
	teacher	Lehrer/Lehrerin
	with	mit; bei →
	it's (= it is)	es ist (er/sie ist; *nicht bei Personen*) →
	she's (= she is)	sie ist
	he's (= he is)	er ist
	we're (= we are)	wir sind

STORY

14	**friend**	Freund/Freundin
	Hi.	Hallo.
	for	für
	maths	Mathe(matik)
	now	nun, jetzt
	open: Open …	öffnen: Öffne … / Öffnet …
	book	Buch; Heft
	please	bitte
	exercise	Übung
	at	bei; an; in
	Thank you. / Thanks.	Danke.
	good at maths	gut in Mathe
15	**girl**	Mädchen
	girlfriend	(feste) Freundin →
	You're right.	Du hast Recht.

What's your name? – I'm Julia.
Where are you from? – I'm from Germany.
How old are you? – I'm 11.

My house is number 6. And *your* house?
– Number 10.

a *badge*

I'm *not* from England. I'm from Germany.

You're *unfriendly.* – No, I'm not. I'm friendly.

a football a *football team*

Mike is a *nice boy*.
– Tom and Martin are nice *boys*, too.

I'm in Class 6A *with* Anna.

Here's a ball. | Here's a school. | Here's a
It's new. | *It's* big. | house.

I	= ich
you	= du, ihr, Sie
he	= er
she	= sie
it	= es (er, sie)
we	= wir
they	= sie

Mark is my friend. Sarah is my *girlfriend*.

I'm sorry. / Sorry.	Tut mir Leid.
Right or wrong?	Richtig oder falsch?

ACTIVE ENGLISH

16	**mum**	Mama, Mutti
	Good afternoon.	Guten Tag. *(nachmittags)*
	Mr	Herr *(vor Namen)* →
	See you.	Bis dann.
	Bye. / Bye-bye.	Tschüs. Wiedersehen.
	Goodbye.	Auf Wiedersehen.
	Good evening.	Guten Abend.
17	**English**	englisch; Englisch; Engländer/Engländerin →
	word	Wort

My teacher is *Mr* Lee.
– And my teacher is Mrs Lee!

PRACTICE PAGES

18	**in my photo**	auf meinem Foto
	Bavaria	Bayern

My *English* name is Susan.
Here's my English badge.
Here's Alan. He's English.

I'm Susan

SPECIAL TOPIC

20	**classroom**	Klassenzimmer
	pupil	Schüler/Schülerin
	lesson	(Unterrichts-)Stunde
	Can we have a …?	Können wir ein/e … haben?
	game	Spiel
	story, stories	Geschichte, Geschichten
	song	Lied
	What's … in English?	Wie (Was) heißt … auf Englisch? →
	German	deutsch; Deutsch; Deutsche/Deutscher →
	listen: Listen.	zuhören: Hör zu. / Hört zu.
	look: Look here.	schauen, sehen: Schau/Schaut (hier)her.
	write: Write …	schreiben: Schreib/t …
21	**pencil-case**	Federmäppchen, Schreibetui
	pen	Füller
	rubber	Radiergummi
	ruler	Lineal
	felt-tip	Filzstift
	biro	Kugelschreiber
	pencil	Bleistift
	bag	Schultasche
	board	Tafel

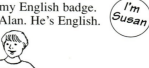

What's "Bleistift" in English, Mary?
– "Pencil."

Is Julia English?
– No, she's *German*.

TIPS

Die vielen neuen englischen Wörter kannst du nicht alle auf einmal lernen. Besser ist, du machst es so:

- Teile dir die Vokabeln in **Abschnitte** von ungefähr 5 bis 8 Wörtern ein und lerne dann abschnittweise.
- Nimm dir **jeden Tag** Zeit, einen Teil zu lernen und einen Teil zu wiederholen.

UNIT TWO VOCABULARY

24	**at home**	zu Hause, daheim
	garage	Garage
	garden	Garten
	some	einige, ein paar
	village	Dorf
	an	ein/eine
25	**family**	Familie →
	her	ihr/ihre
	in front of	vor
	next to	neben →
	mother	Mutter
	dog	Hund
	parent, parents	Elternteil, Eltern
	brother	Bruder
	cat	Katze
	neighbour	Nachbar/Nachbarin
	his	sein/seine
	sister	Schwester
	grandma	Oma, Großmutter
	they aren't (= they are not)	sie sind nicht
26	**the**	der/die/das
	bedroom	Schlafzimmer →
	other	andere, weitere →
	room	Zimmer, Raum
	kitchen	Küche
	living-room	Wohnzimmer
	toilet	Toilette
	bathroom	Badezimmer, Bad
	small	klein
	dad	Papa, Vati
	where	wo; wohin →
	open	offen, geöffnet
	from 8 in the morning till 10 in the evening	von 8 (Uhr) morgens bis 10 (Uhr) abends
	late	spät; zu spät, verspätet
27	**you're lucky**	du hast Glück
	busy	beschäftigt; hektisch, belebt →
	… is/are fun	… macht/machen Spaß →
	Well, …	Nun, …
	thing	Ding, Sache
	free	kostenlos; frei
	Let's go.	Lass/Lasst uns gehen. / Gehen wir. →
	customer	Kunde/Kundin

STORY

28	**always**	immer
	our	unser/unsere
	broken	kaputt, zerbrochen
	TV programme	Fernsehsendung →
	today	heute →
	everything	alles
	Never mind.	Macht nichts. Egal.
	at our house / at Asif's flat	bei uns/Asif (zu Hause)

⚠ **an o**ld house − **a n**ew house

Here's Mike's *family*:

Tibby is *next to* Jessica.

a *bedroom*   a bed

Some pupils in Class 6B are 10.
Other pupils in Class 6B are 11.

> **ZIMMER**
> bedroom
> living-room
> kitchen
> bathroom
> toilet

Tim, w*here* are you? − I'm here.

Dad is *busy* in the kitchen.   The shop is very *busy*.
Football *is fun!* − Yes, but videos *are fun*, too.

We're late.
− You're right. *Let's go.*

The *TV programmes* aren't good *today*.

29	**what**	welche/welcher/welches →
	only	nur, bloß; erst
	minute	Minute
	Just a minute.	Einen Augenblick.
	pound (£)	Pfund *(britisches Geld)* →

I'm at Park School. – *What* class? – Class 6B.

 one *pound*   ten pounds

ACTIVE ENGLISH

30	**phone book**	Telefonbuch →
31	*balcony*	Balkon

a phone (telephone)   a book   a *phone book*

SPECIAL TOPIC

34	**pop**	Popmusik, Pop
	bus	Bus
35	*green*	grün
	bottle	Flasche
	verse	Strophe
	are standing on a wall	stehen auf einer Mauer
	is now about to fall	fällt jetzt gleich hinunter
	no bottles	keine Flaschen

TEST YOURSELF

a **FAMILIE**
mother
?
?
?
?
?

b **EIN „H" IM WORT**
m - - **h** - r = mother
n - - - **h** - - - r = ?
k - - - **h** - n = ?
b - - **h** - - - m = ?
- **h** - - e = ?
- **h** - - e b - - k = ?

c **Ergänze.**
1 Some pupils are in Class 6A. … pupils are in Class 6B.
2 Emma, … are you? – I'm in the kitchen.
3 Mrs Brown is … in the kitchen.
4 A dog … …! – Yes, but cats … …, too.
5 It's late. … … – OK.
6 I'm from London Road. – … number? – Number 6.

TIPS

WORD BOX

Kannst du dir manche Wörter einfach nicht merken? Willst du nur bestimmte Wörter wiederholen? Oder möchtest du einfach mal anders Vokabeln lernen? – Dann brauchst du eine **WORD BOX**, also:

- kleine Kärtchen (oder gleich große Zettel)
- einen passenden Kasten.

Auf die Kärtchen schreibst du vorn das englische Wort, hinten das deutsche. (Es können natürlich auch mehrere Wörter oder ein Satz sein.)

Nun schau dir die Karten einzeln von vorn oder von hinten an. Weißt du noch, wie das Wort in der anderen Sprache heißt?

Ja? Dann stecke das Kärtchen nach hinten in das „OK-Fach" der **WORD BOX**. Nein? Das Kärtchen kommt zurück in das „Fragezeichen-Fach". Beim nächsten Mal schaust du es dir wieder an – bis du dir die Wörter darauf gemerkt hast.

village

Let's go.

spät;
zu spät,
verspätet

UNIT THREE VOCABULARY

38	**there's** (= there is)	da ist, es gibt, es ist →
	there are	da sind, es gibt, es sind →
	window	Fenster, Schaufenster
	board	Tafel
	door	Tür
	cupboard	Schrank
	table	Tisch
	chair	Stuhl
	bag	(Schul-)Tasche, Tüte →
39	**group**	Gruppe
	this	dies/das (hier); diese/dieser/dieses →
	job	Aufgabe; Arbeit, Beruf
	watch	zusehen, sich anschauen
	read	lesen, vorlesen
	listen to	hören, sich anhören
	stand up	aufstehen
	sit down	sich setzen
	do	tun, machen
	Put your hands up.	Hebt die Hände hoch.
	say: O'Grady says	sagen: O'Grady sagt
40	**open day**	Tag der offenen Tür →
	money	Geld
	minibus	Kleinbus
	idea	Idee, Einfall; Ahnung
	have	haben
	match	Spiel, Wettkampf →
	bring	bringen, mitbringen
	sweet	Süßigkeit, Bonbon
	stall	(Verkaufs-)Stand
	plant	Pflanze
	cake	(kleiner) Kuchen →
	lots of	viele; viel
	paint	malen; streichen
	sign	Schild; Zeichen
	make	machen, herstellen
	plan	planen, vorhaben
	Sharon **is painting.**	Sharon malt gerade.
	Some girls **are making** …	Einige Mädchen machen gerade … →
41	**its**	sein/seine; ihr/ihre →
	their	ihr/ihre →
	surprise	Überraschung; Überraschungs-
	letter	Brief
	about	über
	to	zu, nach; an
	wet	nass, feucht
	sponge	Schwamm

STORY

42	**come**	kommen →
	false	falsch
	alarm	Alarm; Alarmanlage
	throw (at)	werfen (nach)

There's a bed in my bedroom.
There are 11 boys or girls in a football team.

bags

This is a cupboard.

The *open day* at our school
  is always a very nice day.

Let's have a football *match* next month.
  – No, let's have a tennis match.

cakes

Sally and Sam *are painting.*
The team? It's good. *Its* name is "Chester City".
The Greens are in *their* garden.

⚠ **it's** = es (er/sie) ist
  its = sein/seine; ihr/ihre

⚠ **their** = ihr/ihre
 they're = sie sind

Come here, Pluto!

IM ZIMMER
door
table
chair
cupboard
bed
window

IM UNTER-RICHT
listen
look
write
read
watch
listen to
stand up
sit down

MEIN, DEIN, …
my
your
his
her
its
our
their

3

What's the matter?	Was ist los?	
car	Auto	
red	rot	
on	an, eingeschaltet →	
43 **stand**	stehen	
too late	zu spät →	
me	mir/mich	

Listen! The walkman is *on*.

The shops aren't open now. It's *too late*.

ACTIVE ENGLISH

44 **Let's ride our bikes.**	Lass uns Rad fahren.
afternoon	Nachmittag
dialogue	Dialog, Gespräch
45 *postcard*	Postkarte, Ansichtskarte
favourite	Lieblings-
Best wishes, …	Viele Grüße …
Dear …,	Liebe …, / Lieber …,

DER TAG
morning
afternoon
evening

PRACTICE PAGES

47 **action**	Handlung, Tätigkeit

SPECIAL TOPIC

48 **colour**	Farbe
favourite	Lieblings- →
blue	blau
yellow	gelb
green	grün
black	schwarz
white	weiß
brown	braun
pink	rosa, pink
What colour is …?	Welche Farbe hat …? →
number plate	Nummernschild
jelly baby	*(eine Art)* Gummibärchen
49 *balloon*	Luftballon, Ballon
over our town	über unserer Stadt
verse	Strophe
Pop!	Peng!
one balloon is down	ein Luftballon ist unten
all	alle

My *favourite* TV programme is "Chester Road". My favourite book is "The cat", and my favourite teacher is Mr Lee.

FARBEN
red
yellow
blue
green
pink
brown
black
white

What colour is your cat?
– She's black.

TEST YOURSELF

a **LET'S …**
have a football match.
? sweets for a sweet stall.
? a sign.
? a poster.
? a surprise stall.
? a sponge at a teacher.
? our bikes.

b **OA – OO – OU?**
b - - rd = b**oa**rd
cupb - - rd = ?
gr - - p = ?
ab - - t = ?
t - - late = ?
aftern - - n = ?
col - - r = ?

c Ergänze.
1 … a pen in my pencil-case.
2 … … 20 boys and girls in my class.
3 The house? It's big. … rooms are big, too.
4 Asif and Dave are at … stall.
5 The pupils aren't at school now. It's … …
6 My … TV programme is "The quiz".
7 … … … your new T-shirt? – It's pink.

UNIT FOUR VOCABULARY

52	**I'm hungry.**	Ich habe Hunger.
	child, children	Kind, Kinder
	eat	essen
	fish and chips	Fisch und Pommes frites
	cheap	billig, preiswert
	take-away …	… zum Mitnehmen
	meal	Mahlzeit, Speise, (zubereitetes) Essen →
	chip shop	Pommes-frites-Bude →
	food	Essen; Lebensmittel; Futter
	milk shake	Milchmixgetränk
	drink	Getränk
53	**What about …?**	Wie wäre es mit …? Was ist mit …? →
	father	Vater
	great	toll, großartig
	burger	Frikadelle; Hamburger
	roll	Brötchen
	cheese	Käse
	I'm thirsty.	Ich habe Durst.
	lemonade	Limonade
	bottle	Flasche
	a bottle of milk	eine Flasche Milch
	carton	Karton, Becher
	ice-cream	(Speise-)Eis
	orange juice	Orangensaft →
	apple juice	Apfelsaft →
54	**banana**	Banane
	chocolate	(Trink-)Schokolade
	on TV	im Fernsehen →
	cable TV	Kabelfernsehen
	sandwich	Sandwich *(belegtes Brot)*
	yoghurt	Joghurt
	crisps	Kartoffelchips
55	**empty**	leer
	radio	Radio

STORY

56	**was**	war
	ill	krank
	had	hatte / hatten
	said	sagte / sagten
	cooking	Kochen
	put	stellen; legen; *(an einen Platz)* tun →
	on	auf →
	wash up	abwaschen, spülen
57	**after**	nach →
	sauce	Soße
	American	amerikanisch; Amerikaner/in

ACTIVE ENGLISH

58	**who**	wer →
	daughter	Tochter

⚠ one child – two child**ren**

I'm hungry. Let's eat a nice *meal*.
– Great. Let's go to the *chip shop!*

I'm hungry. *What about* a hot dog?
– OK. What about Sam? Is he
  hungry, too?

ESSEN
I'm hungry.
Let's eat.
meal
take-away meal
snack
food

an orange   an apple   a bottle of *orange juice* and
                           a bottle of *apple juice*

What's *on TV*? – A football match.

⚠ **chips** = Pommes frites
  crisps = Kartoffelchips

Put the sandwiches *on* the
  kitchen table, please.

WO?
in front of
next to
above
in
on

After 10 minutes I said, "Let's go now."

Who are you?
– I'm the new pupil.

⚠ **who** = wer
  where = wo

son	Sohn
why	warum →
aunt	Tante
uncle	Onkel
camera	Fotoapparat, Kamera
grandmother	Großmutter
grandfather	Großvater
59 *family tree*	Stammbaum (der Familie)
cousin	Cousin/Cousine, Vetter
crispies	*knusprige kleine Kuchen*
dish	Schüssel
melt	schmelzen
with hot water	mit heißem Wasser
microwave	Mikrowelle
put in	hinzufügen
mix	mischen
Eat them when they're cold.	Iss sie, wenn sie kalt sind.
vanilla	Vanille
glass	(Trink-)Glas
popular	beliebt
nicer than	schöner als, besser als

Why is mum in bed?
– She's ill.

> **FAMILIE**
> grandmother
> grandfather
> parents
> (mother, father)
> children
> (daughter, son)
> aunt
> uncle

SPECIAL TOPIC

62 **pence (p)**	Pence *(britisches Geld)*
How much is …?	Was kostet …? – Er/Sie/Es
– It's £ … .	kostet … Pfund. →
calculator	Taschenrechner
Can I have …, please?	Kann ich bitte … haben?
postcard	Postkarte, Ansichtskarte
magazine	Zeitschrift →
63 **pocket-money**	Taschengeld
£3 a week	3 Pfund pro Woche
month	Monat
euro (€)	Euro →
cent	Cent →
hot cross bun	*(eine Art)* Rosinenbrötchen
one a penny	eins für einen Penny
if	wenn
no	kein/e
give them to …	gib sie …

How much is a lemonade at the restaurant?
– *It's £1.*

magazines

My pocket-money is four *euros* and
fifty *cents* a week.

> day
> week
> month

T E S T   Y O U R S E L F

a
GETRÄNKE	
milk shake	
?	?
?	?

b
PAARE	
hungry	– thirsty
a drink	– ?
daughter	– ?
uncle	– ?

c Ergänze.
1 I'm hungry. What … a hamburger?
2 What's … …? – A western.
3 … the drinks on the table, please.
4 … is dad at home? – He's ill.

T I P S

Manche Wörter behältst du besser, wenn du sie im ganzen Satz siehst. Die kleine blaue Seitenzahl sagt dir, wo ein Wort zum ersten Mal vorkommt. Schau dort nach und schreibe den ganzen Satz zu dem Wort auf deiner **WORD BOX**-Karte.

> was
>
> Mrs Kelly was ill.

UNIT FIVE VOCABULARY

66 **buy** · kaufen
toy · Spielzeug →
car-boot sale · (eine Art) Trödelmarkt
in a field · auf einem Feld
near · in der Nähe (von); nah
second-hand · aus zweiter Hand, gebraucht
car-boot · Kofferraum
people · Leute, Menschen
often · oft
at the weekend · am Wochenende
tool · Werkzeug
picture · Bild, Foto →
market · Markt
meet · (sich) treffen (mit); kennen lernen →
there · da, dort; dahin, dorthin →
67 **no** · kein/keine
sell · verkaufen
them · ihnen/sie →
help · helfen
animal home · Tierheim →
train · Zug, Eisenbahn
building set · Baukasten
doll · Puppe
farm set · Spielzeugbauernhof
kite · (Papier-)Drachen
play · spielen
leave · lassen; verlassen, weggehen von
68 **break** · (zer)brechen, kaputtmachen
run · rennen, laufen
place · Ort, Platz, Stelle
69 **want** · wollen
that · das; der/die/das (da) →
cost · kosten →

STORY

70 **need** · brauchen
special · besondere/besonderer/besonderes
expensive · teuer
us · uns
enough · genug
man, men · Mann, Männer
Excuse me, … · Entschuldigen Sie, …
wife · Ehefrau
collect · sammeln, einsammeln
first · erste/erster/erstes
every · jede/jeder/jedes →
battery · Batterie
71 **over there** · da drüben, dort drüben
again · (schon) wieder, noch einmal
like · mögen, gern haben →
price · (Kauf-)Preis
him · ihm/ihn →

There are lots of *toys* in a toy-shop.

There's a little cat in Nick's *picture*.

At the weekend I *meet* my friends.

Where's the dog? – It's *there*, in front of the cupboard.

Let's buy some CDs.
– Good idea. Let's buy *them* at "Cool's CDs".

There are lots of animals in an *animal home*.

That's my sister, look!

The walkman *costs* £10.

EINKAUFEN
shop
money
How much is …?
It's £1.
sell
buy
cost
expensive
cheap
price

⚠ one man – two men

Every weekend there's a car-boot sale near York.

I *like* animals. And you?

Robbie is a nice boy. I like *him*.

5

ACTIVE ENGLISH

72	**sport**	Sport, Sportart →
73	*This is the way I pump the tyre.*	So pumpe ich den Reifen auf.
	then	dann
	higher	höher
	puncture	Loch im Reifen
	slower	langsamer
	lower	niedriger
	scream (for)	schreien (nach)
	all	alle; ganz
	cow	Kuh
	love	lieben
	with all my heart	von ganzem Herzen
	she gives me cream	sie gibt mir Sahne
	with all her might	mit ihrer ganzen Kraft
	to eat	um zu essen
	apple tart	Apfelkuchen
	singer	Sänger/Sängerin
	I think	ich finde, ich meine
	all	alle
	of	von
	music	Musik
	look at	(sich) ansehen →
	find	finden

Basketball and jogging are my favourite *sports*.

SPECIAL TOPIC

76	**time**	Zeit; Uhrzeit
	It's 2 o'clock.	Es ist 2 Uhr.
	What time is it?	Wie spät ist es?
	when	wann →
	at 10 o'clock	um 10 Uhr
77	*mouse*	Maus
	ran up	rannte hinauf
	clock	Uhr
	struck	schlug
	ran down	rannte hinab

Mum, let's *look at* the nice bikes over there.

When's the car-boot sale?
– At the weekend.

FRAGEWÖRTER
Who? = Wer?
What? = Was?
When? = Wann?
Where? = Wo?
Why? = Warum?

TIPS

Partnerspiele mit der WORD BOX

- Deine Partnerin / Dein Partner liest das **deutsche Wort** auf dem Kärtchen vor. Wie heißt es auf Englisch? Wenn du es weißt, bekommst du das Kärtchen und darfst die nächste Frage stellen.
  Sonst ist deine Partnerin / dein Partner noch einmal dran.

- Deine Partnerin / Dein Partner liest das **englische Wort** auf dem Kärtchen vor. Wie heißt der Satz dazu?

- Deine Partnerin / Dein Partner liest den **englischen Satz** auf dem Kärtchen vor, lässt dabei aber das Wort aus, das oben auf dem Kärtchen steht. Wie heißt das fehlende englische Wort?

Mit einem Cassettenrecorder kannst du alle diese Spiele auch allein machen.
Du musst nur beim Aufnehmen immer eine ausreichend lange Pause für deine Antwort lassen.

UNIT SIX VOCABULARY

80 **work** — arbeiten; funktionieren
go to the shops — einkaufen gehen →
sometimes — manchmal
clothes — Kleidung, Kleider →
watch TV — fernsehen
visit — besuchen; besichtigen
cinema — Kino
swim — schwimmen
never — nie, niemals
81 **Monday** — Montag
in spring — im Frühling
summer — Sommer
holiday — Feiertag; Ferien, Urlaub
long — lang
interesting — interessant →
walk — wandern; (zu Fuß) gehen
in the country — auf dem Land
zoo — Zoo
seaside — Küste
sports matches — Sportveranstaltungen
fun park — Freizeitpark, Erlebnispark
stay — bleiben
83 **on Monday** — am Montag; montags
cousin — Cousin/Cousine, Vetter
live — wohnen, leben →
farm — Bauernhof, Farm
question — Frage
answer to — Antwort auf

STORY

84 Claire **visited** — Claire besuchte
laugh — lachen
want to go — gehen wollen →
take photos — Fotos machen, fotografieren
of — von
cow — Kuh →
chicken — Huhn →
pig — Schwein →
sheep — Schaf, Schafe →
cereal — Getreide
potato, potatoes — Kartoffel, Kartoffeln
ride on the tractor — auf dem Traktor mitfahren
modern — modern
sad — traurig
85 **feed** — füttern, zu fressen geben
different from — anders als →
far — weit
museum — Museum
opposite — Gegenteil →
plural — Plural, Mehrzahl

ACTIVE ENGLISH

86 **play sport** — Sport treiben
model — Modell; Nachbildung

My father always *goes to the shops* at the weekend.

Great *clothes!*
– Yes, and they're cheap.

WIE OFT?
always
often
sometimes
never

I like holidays. We often do *interesting* things.

Do you *live* in Chester? – No, I don't. I live in York.

I *want to* stay here. I don't want to go with you.

cows   *chickens*   *pigs*   *sheep*

⚠ one sheep
  two sheep

Your dog is *different from* my dog.

The *opposite* of "cheap"
is "expensive".

AUF DEM LAND
in the country
village
farm
tractor
potato
cereal

6

87 **I like skateboarding.** Ich fahre gern Skateboard.
  skateboarding Skateboardfahren
  swimming Schwimmen →
  skating Schlittschuh-, Rollschuh-
    laufen
  the names of the sports die Namen der Sportarten

James often swims.
He likes *swimming*.

SPECIAL TOPIC

90 **weekday** Wochentag
  Tuesday Dienstag
  Wednesday Mittwoch
  Thursday Donnerstag
  Friday Freitag
  get up aufstehen
  have a wash sich waschen
  have breakfast frühstücken →
  I clean my teeth. Ich putze mir die Zähne.
  count zählen
  Saturday Samstag, Sonnabend
  Sunday Sonntag
  come home nach Hause kommen
91 *all the year* das ganze Jahr
  verse Strophe
  when wenn
  feel very slow sich sehr träge fühlen
  then dann
  quick schnell
  put on things Sachen anziehen
  sing singen
  eat up aufessen
  talk reden, sprechen
  much viel
  run for the bus rennen, um den Bus zu
    bekommen
  at the end of the day am Ende des Tages
  a few hours later ein paar Stunden später
  it all starts again es fängt alles wieder (von
    vorn) an

Pamela *has breakfast* at 7.00.
This is her breakfast.

WOCHENTAGE
Monday
Tuesday
Wednesday
Thursday
Friday
Saturday
Sunday

come home
go home
stay at home

TEST YOURSELF

a **HE'S/SHE'S/IT'S …**
sad
?
?
?
?
?

b **ZWEI WÖRTER**
watch TV
? photos
? sport
? up
? breakfast
? home

c Ergänze.
1 My mother always … … … … on Tuesdays.
2 This shop has great …! – Yes, but they're expensive.
3 Do you … in Germany? – Yes, I do.
4 I want to read. I don't … … watch TV.
5 Your cat is … … my cat.
6 The … of "new" is "old".
7 I often swim. I'm good at …

UNIT SEVEN VOCABULARY

94	**centre**	Zentrum, Mitte
	can	können, dürfen →
	supermarket	Supermarkt
	library	Bücherei
	pet shop	Kleintierhandlung, Zoohandlung
	sports centre	Sportzentrum →
96	**go to town**	in die (Innen-)Stadt gehen
	young	jung
	wallpaper	Tapete
	curtain	Vorhang, Gardine
	cushion	Kissen
	I'm bored	ich langweile mich →
	then	dann
97	**next**	nächste/nächster/nächstes →
	The room **will** have …	Das Zimmer wird … haben.
	It'll (= it will) have new curtains.	Es wird neue Vorhänge haben. →
	be	sein
	tomorrow	morgen →
	park	parken
	car park	Parkhaus, (großer) Parkplatz
	full of cars	voller Autos →
	sure	sicher →
	shirt	Hemd
	We won't (= will not) have time.	Wir werden keine Zeit haben.
	careful	vorsichtig; sorgfältig →
	the cheapest	am billigsten
	market hall	Markthalle

STORY

98	**Come on!**	Komm schon! Los!
	all	alle; alles
	wallet	Brieftasche
	clock	Uhr
99	We'll be late.	Wir werden zu spät kommen.
	credit card	Kreditkarte

ACTIVE ENGLISH

100	**What would you like?**	Was hätten Sie gern?
	I'd like (= I would like) …	Ich hätte gern … / Ich möchte … →
	Here you are.	Hier, bitte. →
	Anything else?	Sonst noch etwas?
	woman, women	Frau, Frauen
	size	Größe
101	*chain*	Kette

We *can* go to the cinema on Saturday. – Super!

Tennis is a sport. You can play it at a *sports centre*.

go to the shops
go to school
go to town
go to bed
go home

Mum, *I'm bored*. What can I do?

Dad, can we go to the match *next* week? – OK.

Pam and I will go to the match next week. *We'll* have lots of fun.

Today is Monday. *Tomorrow* is Tuesday.

IN DER STADT
market
supermarket
cinema
library
museum
car park
sports centre
restaurant

Look at that shop. It's *full of* toys! Where's your sister?
 – I'm not *sure*.

Be *careful* with my CDs, please.

KLEIDUNG
jeans
pullover
shirt
T-shirt
sweatshirt

I'd like a bottle of milk, please.
 – *Here you are.*

⚠ one woman
two women

ONE – TWO
one man –
 two men
one woman –
 two women
one child –
 two children

7

SPECIAL TOPIC

104	**year**	Jahr; Jahrgang →
	January	Januar
	February	Februar
	March	März
	April	April
	May	Mai
	June	Juni
	July	Juli
	August	August
	September	September
	October	Oktober
	November	November
	December	Dezember
	Britain	Großbritannien
	New Year's Day	Neujahrstag
	Thanksgiving Day	Erntedankfest
	Christmas Day	der erste Weihnachtstag
	Independence Day	Unabhängigkeitstag
	Guy Fawkes Night	Guy-Fawkes-Nacht
	in January	im Januar
105	**season**	Jahreszeit →
	autumn	Herbst
	winter	Winter
	calendar calypso	„Kalender-Calypso"

Laura is 14 *years* old.
At school she's in Year 9.

> day
> week
> month
> year

WANN?
at 10 o'clock
today
tomorrow
at the weekend
on Monday
next month
in January

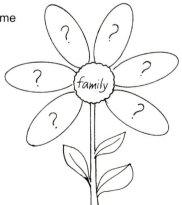

What's your favourite *season*?
– Summer!

DAS JAHR
spring
summer
autumn
winter

T I P S

Die Wortblume

Zeichnest du gern? Dann zeichne doch einmal eine „Wortblume".

Du suchst zuerst einen allgemeinen Begriff und schreibst ihn in die Mitte der Blume, z. B. den Begriff *rooms*.
Dann musst du überlegen (oder auf den *Vocabulary*-Seiten nachschlagen):
Welche Wörter passen zu diesem Begriff? Weiß ich, wie sie auf Englisch heißen?
Diese englischen Wörter schreibst du in die Blütenblätter der Wortblume, bei *rooms* zum Beispiel *bathroom* und *kitchen* (Du kennst noch mehr!).

Und so könnte der Anfang deiner *rooms*-Wortblume dann aussehen:

Versuche auch einmal, eine *family*-Wortblume oder eine *places*-Wortblume zu zeichnen.
Die „blauen" Kästen auf den *Vocabulary*-Seiten helfen dir dabei.

EXTRA PAGES VOCABULARY

Merry Christmas! Happy New Year!

108
Merry Christmas!	Fröhliche Weihnachten!
Happy New Year!	Glückliches neues Jahr!
holiday	Feiertag
Britain	Großbritannien
America	Amerika
British	britisch
Christmas food	Weihnachtsessen
Christmas card	Weihnachtskarte
present	Geschenk
on Christmas Day	am ersten Weihnachtstag
letter	Brief
Father Christmas	der Weihnachtsmann
Christmas cracker	Knallbonbon
joke	Witz, Scherz
hat	Hut

109
Make …	Mache …
Best wishes for …	Mit den besten Wünschen für …
With love from …	Mit lieben Grüßen (von) …
we wish	wir wünschen
glad tidings we bring	frohe Botschaft bringen wir
kin	Familie, Verwandtschaft

presents

Christmas cracker

Bikes and boxes

110
box	Kiste, Kasten
puncture	Reifenpanne
weekend	Wochenende
picnic	Picknick
there	da, dort
long	lang
journey	Fahrt, Reise
meet	sich treffen
sandwich	Sandwich *(belegtes Brot)*
drink	Getränk
I can take …	ich kann … mitnehmen
tool	Werkzeug
on Saturday	am Samstag

A PICNIC

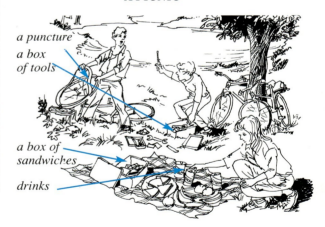

a puncture
a box of tools
a box of sandwiches
drinks

Where's my bike?

112	problem	Problem
	without	ohne
	tea	Tee
	so	also
	went	ging / gingen, fuhr / fuhren
	of course	natürlich, selbstverständlich
	joke	Witz, Scherz
	behind	hinter
	were	waren
	after school	nach der Schule
	police station	Polizeiwache
	didn't see	sah nicht
	auction	Versteigerung
113	didn't have	hatte nicht
	soon	bald
	back	zurück
	first	zuerst
	early	früh
	present	Geschenk
	bike lock	Fahrradschloß

a police station

Dictionary

Alphabetische Liste der Wörter aus Band 1 (Englisch – Deutsch)

A

a [ə] ein/eine; **£3 a week** 3 Pfund pro Woche

about [ə'baʊt] über; **What about …?** Wie wäre es mit …? Was ist mit …?

above [ə'bʌv] über

action ['ækʃn] Handlung, Tätigkeit

after ['ɑːftə] nach

afternoon ['ɑːftə'nuːn] Nachmittag; **Good afternoon.** Guten Tag. *(nachmittags)*; **in the afternoon(s)** nachmittags; am Nachmittag

again [ə'gen] (schon) wieder; noch einmal

alarm [ə'lɑːm] Alarm; Alarmanlage

all [ɔːl] alle; alles

always ['ɔːlweɪz] immer

am [æm]: **I am** ich bin

American [ə'merɪkən] amerikanisch; Amerikaner/Amerikanerin

an [ən] ein/eine

and [ænd, ənd] und

animal ['ænɪməl] Tier; **animal home** Tierheim

answer ['ɑːnsə]: **answer (to)** Antwort (auf)

anything ['eniθɪŋ]: **Anything else?** Sonst noch etwas?

apple ['æpl] Apfel

April ['eɪprəl] April

are [ɑː]: **you are** du bist; ihr seid; Sie sind; **we are** wir sind; **they are** sie sind

at [æt, ət] bei; an; in; **at home** zu Hause, daheim; **at our house / at Asif's flat** bei uns (zu Hause) / bei Asif (zu Hause); **at school** in der Schule; **at 10 o'clock** um 10 Uhr; **at the weekend** am Wochenende

August ['ɔːgəst] August

aunt [ɑːnt] Tante

autumn ['ɔːtəm] Herbst

B

badge [bædʒ] Abzeichen; Anstecker, Button

bag [bæg] Tasche, Schultasche, Tüte

ball [bɔːl] Ball

banana [bə'nɑːnə] Banane

bathroom ['bɑːθruːm] Badezimmer

battery ['bætəri] Batterie

Bavaria [bə'veəriə] Bayern

be [biː] sein

bed [bed] Bett; **go to bed** ins Bett gehen

bedroom ['bedruːm] Schlafzimmer

big [bɪg] groß

bike [baɪk] Fahrrad; **ride a bike** (mit dem) Rad fahren

biro ['baɪrəʊ] Kugelschreiber

black [blæk] schwarz

blue [bluː] blau

board [bɔːd] Tafel

book [bʊk] Buch; Heft

bored [bɔːd] gelangweilt; **I'm bored** ich langweile mich

bottle ['bɒtl] Flasche

boy [bɔɪ] Junge

break [breɪk] brechen, zerbrechen, kaputtmachen

breakfast ['brekfəst] Frühstück; **have breakfast** frühstücken

bring [brɪŋ] bringen, mitbringen

Britain ['brɪtn] Großbritannien

broken ['brəʊkən] gebrochen, zerbrochen, kaputt

brother ['brʌðə] Bruder

brown [braʊn] braun

building set ['bɪldɪŋset] Baukasten

burger ['bɜːgə] Frikadelle; Hamburger

bus [bʌs] Bus

busy ['bɪzi] beschäftigt; hektisch, belebt

but [bʌt] aber

buy [baɪ] kaufen

Bye. / Bye-bye. [baɪ, baɪ'baɪ] Tschüs. Wiedersehen.

C

cable TV [keɪbltiː'viː] Kabelfernsehen

café ['kæfeɪ] Café

cake [keɪk] (kleiner) Kuchen

calculator ['kælkjuleɪtə] Taschenrechner

camera ['kæmrə] Fotoapparat, Kamera

can [kæn, kən] können, dürfen; **Can we have a …?** Können wir

ein/e … haben? **Can I have …, please?** Kann ich bitte … haben? **I can't** [kɑːnt] **(= cannot** ['kænɒt]**)** ich kann nicht, ich darf nicht

car [kɑː] Auto; **car park** Parkhaus, *(großer)* Parkplatz

car-boot ['kɑːbuːt] Kofferraum; **car-boot sale** ['kɑːbuːtseɪl] *(eine Art)* Trödelmarkt

careful ['keəfəl] vorsichtig; sorgfältig

carton ['kɑːtn] Karton, Becher

cassette [kə'set] Cassette

cat [kæt] Katze

CD [siː'diː] CD

cent [sent] Cent

centre ['sentə] Zentrum, Mitte

cereal ['sɪərɪəl] Getreide

chair [tʃeə] Stuhl

cheap [tʃiːp] billig, preiswert

cheese [tʃiːz] Käse

cheeseburger ['tʃiːzbɜːgə] Cheeseburger

chicken ['tʃɪkɪn] Huhn; (Brat-)Hähnchen

child, children [tʃaɪld, 'tʃɪldrən] Kind, Kinder

chip shop ['tʃɪpʃɒp] Pommes-frites-Bude

chips [tʃɪps] Pommes frites

chocolate ['tʃɒklət] Trinkschokolade; Schokolade

Christmas ['krɪsməs] Weihnachten; **Christmas Day** der erste Weihnachtstag

cinema ['sɪnəmə] Kino

class [klɑːs] Klasse

classroom ['klɑːsruːm] Klassenzimmer

clean [kliːn]: **I clean my teeth.** Ich putze mir die Zähne.

clock [klɒk] Uhr

clothes [kləʊðz] Kleidung, Kleider

cola ['kəʊlə] Cola

collect [kə'lekt] sammeln, einsammeln

colour ['kʌlə] Farbe; **What colour is …?** Welche Farbe hat …?

come [kʌm] kommen; **Come on!** Komm schon! Los!

comic ['kɒmɪk] Comic(heft)

computer [kəm'pjuːtə] Computer, Rechner

cooking ['kʊkɪŋ] Kochen
cost [kɒst] *(Geld)* kosten
count [kaʊnt] zählen
country ['kʌntri] Land; **in the country** auf dem Land
cousin ['kʌzn] Cousin/Cousine, Vetter
cow [kaʊ] Kuh
credit card ['kredɪtkɑːd] Kreditkarte
crisps [krɪsps] Kartoffelchips
cupboard ['kʌbəd] Schrank
curtain ['kɜːtn] Vorhang, Gardine
cushion ['kʊʃn] Kissen
customer ['kʌstəmə] Kunde/Kundin

D

dad [dæd] Papa, Vati
daughter ['dɔːtə] Tochter
day [deɪ] Tag; **open day** Tag der offenen Tür
December [dɪ'sembə] Dezember
dialogue ['daɪəlɒg] Dialog, Gespräch
different ['dɪfrənt] andere/anderer/anderes; verschieden, anders; **different from** anders als
do [duː] tun, machen
dog [dɒg] Hund
doll [dɒl] Puppe
door [dɔː] Tür
drink [drɪŋk] Getränk

E

eat [iːt] essen
else [els]: **Anything else?** Sonst noch etwas?
empty ['empti] leer
England ['ɪŋglənd] England
English ['ɪŋglɪʃ] englisch; Englisch; Engländer/Engländerin
enough [ɪ'nʌf] genug
euro (€) ['jʊərəʊ] Euro
Europe ['jʊərəp] Europa
evening ['iːvnɪŋ] Abend; **Good evening.** Guten Abend. **in the evening(s)** abends; am Abend
every ['evri] jede/jeder/jedes
everything ['evriθɪŋ] alles
excuse [ɪk'skjuːz]: **Excuse me, ...** Entschuldigen Sie, ...
exercise ['eksəsaɪz] Übung
expensive [ɪk'spensɪv] teuer

F

false [fɔːls] falsch
family ['fæmli] Familie
fan [fæn] Fan, Anhänger/Anhängerin
far [fɑː] weit
farm [fɑːm] Bauernhof, Farm; **farm set** ['fɑːmset] Spielzeugbauernhof
father ['fɑːðə] Vater
favourite ['feɪvrət] Lieblings-
February ['februəri] Februar
feed [fiːd] füttern, zu fressen geben
felt-tip ['felttɪp] Filzstift
field [fiːld] Feld, Wiese
film [fɪlm] Film
find [faɪnd] finden
first [fɜːst] erste/erster/erstes
fish [fɪʃ] Fisch, Fische; **fish and chips** Fisch und Pommes frites
flat [flæt] Wohnung; **At Asif's flat** bei Asif (zu Hause)
food [fuːd] Essen; Lebensmittel; Futter
football ['fʊtbɔːl] Fußball
for [fɔː, fə] für
free [friː] frei; kostenlos; **free time** Freizeit
Friday ['fraɪdeɪ, 'fraɪdi] Freitag
friend [frend] Freund/Freundin
friendly ['frendli] freundlich
from [frɒm, frəm] von; aus; **from 8 till 10** von 8 (Uhr) bis 10 (Uhr)
front [frʌnt]: **in front of** vor
full [fʊl]: **full of cars** voller Autos
fun [fʌn] Spaß; **... is/are fun.** ... macht/machen Spaß. **fun park** Freizeitpark, Erlebnispark, Vergnügungspark

G

game [geɪm] Spiel
garage ['gærɑːʒ] Garage
garden ['gɑːdn] Garten
German ['dʒɜːmən] deutsch; Deutsch; Deutsche/Deutscher
Germany ['dʒɜːməni] Deutschland
get up [get'ʌp] aufstehen
girl [gɜːl] Mädchen
girlfriend ['gɜːlfrend] (feste) Freundin
go [gəʊ] gehen, fahren; **go to bed** ins Bett gehen; **go to school** zur Schule gehen; **go to the shops** einkaufen gehen; **go to town** in die Stadt gehen

good [gʊd] gut; **good at** gut in, geschickt in; **Good afternoon.** Guten Tag. *(nachmittags)*; **Good evening.** Guten Abend. **Good morning.** Guten Morgen. **Goodbye.** [gʊd'baɪ] Auf Wiedersehen.
grandfather ['grænfɑːðə] Großvater
grandma ['grænmɑː] Oma, Großmutter
grandmother ['grænmʌðə] Großmutter
great [greɪt] toll, großartig
green [griːn] grün
group [gruːp] Gruppe

H

had [hæd] hatte/hatten
Hallo. [hə'ləʊ] Hallo. Guten Tag.
hamburger ['hæmbɜːgə] Hamburger
have [hæv] haben; **have a wash** sich waschen; **have breakfast** frühstücken
he [hiː] er
help [help] helfen
her [hɜː] ihr/ihre
here [hɪə] hier; hierhin/hierher; **Here you are.** Hier, bitte.
Hi. [haɪ] Hallo.
him [hɪm] ihm/ihn
his [hɪz] sein/seine
hobby ['hɒbi] Hobby
hockey ['hɒki] Hockey
holiday ['hɒlədeɪ] Feiertag; Ferien, Urlaub
home [həʊm] 1. Heim, Zuhause; 2. nach Hause, heim; **at home** zu Hause, daheim
hot dog ['hɒt'dɒg] Hot Dog
house [haʊs] Haus; **at our house** bei uns (zu Hause)
how [haʊ] wie; **How much is/are ...?** Was kostet/kosten ...? **How old are you?** Wie alt bist du?
hungry ['hʌŋgri] hungrig; **I'm hungry.** Ich habe Hunger.

I

I [aɪ] ich; **I'd** [aɪd] **(= I would): I'd like ...** Ich möchte ... / Ich hätte gern ...
ice-cream [aɪs'kriːm] (Speise-)Eis

idea [aɪˈdɪə] Idee, Einfall; Ahnung
ill [ɪl] krank
in [ɪn] in; **in English** auf Englisch; **in front of** vor; **in January** im Januar; **in my photo** auf meinem Foto; **in the country** auf dem Land; **in the morning(s) / in the afternoon(s) / in the evening(s)** morgens/nachmittags/abends; am Morgen / am Nachmittag / am Abend; **in town** in der (Innen-)Stadt
Independence Day [ɪndɪˈpendənsdeɪ] Unabhängigkeitstag
interesting [ˈɪntrəstɪŋ] interessant
is [ɪz]: **he/she/it is** er/sie/es ist
it [ɪt] es (er/sie; *nicht bei Personen*)
its [ɪts] sein/seine; ihr/ihre

January [ˈdʒænjuəri] Januar
jeans [dʒiːnz] Jeans
jelly baby [ˈdʒelibeɪbi] *(eine Art)* Gummibärchen
job [dʒɒb] Arbeit, Beruf; Aufgabe
juice [dʒuːs] Saft
July [dʒuˈlaɪ] Juli
June [dʒuːn] Juni
just [dʒʌst]: **Just a minute.** Einen Augenblick.

ketchup [ˈketʃəp] Ketchup
kitchen [ˈkɪtʃɪn] Küche
kite [kaɪt] (Papier-)Drachen

late [leɪt] spät; zu spät, verspätet; **We'll be late.** Wir werden zu spät kommen.
laugh [lɑːf] lachen
leave [liːv] (liegen/stehen) lassen; verlassen, weggehen von, abfahren
lemonade [leməˈneɪd] Limonade
lesson [ˈlesn] (Unterrichts-)Stunde
let [let]: **Let's go!** Lass/Lasst uns gehen. / Gehen wir!
letter [ˈletə] Brief
library [ˈlaɪbrəri] Bücherei

like [laɪk] mögen, gern haben; **I like skateboarding.** Ich fahre gern Skateboard. **I'd like …** Ich möchte … / Ich hätte gern …; **What would you like?** Was hätten Sie gern?
listen [ˈlɪsn] zuhören; **listen to** hören, sich anhören
live [lɪv] wohnen, leben
living-room [ˈlɪvɪŋruːm] Wohnzimmer
long [lɒŋ] lang
look [lʊk] schauen, sehen; **look at** (sich) ansehen
lot [lɒt]: **lots of** viele; viel
lucky [ˈlʌki] glücklich; **you're lucky** du hast Glück

magazine [mægəˈziːn] Zeitschrift
make [meɪk] machen, herstellen
man, men [mæn, men] Mann, Männer
March [mɑːtʃ] März
market [ˈmɑːkɪt] Markt; **market hall** [ˈmɑːkɪthɔːl] Markthalle
match [mætʃ] Spiel, Wettkampf
maths [mæθs] Mathe(matik)
matter [ˈmætə]: **What's the matter?** Was ist los?
May [meɪ] Mai
me [miː] mir/mich
meal [miːl] Mahlzeit, Speise, (zubereitetes) Essen
meet [miːt] (sich) treffen (mit); kennen lernen
milk [mɪlk] Milch; **milk shake** [ˈmɪlkʃeɪk] Milchmixgetränk
mind [ˈmaind]: **Never mind.** Macht nichts. Egal.
minibus [ˈmɪnibʌs] Kleinbus
minute [ˈmɪnɪt] Minute; **Just a minute.** Einen Augenblick.
model [ˈmɒdl] Modell; Nachbildung
modern [ˈmɒdən] modern
Monday [ˈmʌndeɪ, ˈmʌndi] Montag; **on Monday** am Montag; montags
money [ˈmʌni] Geld
month [mʌnθ] Monat
morning [ˈmɔːnɪŋ] Morgen, Vormittag; **Good morning.** Guten Morgen. **in the morning(s)** morgens, vormittags; am Morgen, am Vormittag
mother [ˈmʌðə] Mutter
mountain bike [ˈmaʊntənbaɪk] Mountainbike
Mr [ˈmɪstə] Herr *(vor Namen)*

Mrs [ˈmɪsɪz] Frau *(vor Namen)*
much [mʌtʃ]: **How much is/are …?** Was kostet/kosten …?
mum [mʌm] Mama, Mutti
museum [mjuˈziːəm] Museum
music [ˈmjuːzɪk] Musik
my [maɪ] mein/meine

name [neɪm] Name
near [nɪə] in der Nähe (von); nah
need [niːd] brauchen
neighbour [ˈneɪbə] Nachbar/Nachbarin
never [ˈnevə] nie, niemals; **Never mind.** Macht nichts. Egal.
new [njuː] neu; **New Year's Day** Neujahrstag
next [nekst] nächste/nächster/nächstes
next to [ˈnekstu, ˈnekstə] neben
nice [naɪs] nett; schön
night [naɪt] Nacht, (später) Abend
no [nəʊ] 1. nein; 2. kein/keine
not [nɒt] nicht
November [nəʊˈvembə] November
now [naʊ] nun, jetzt
number [ˈnʌmbə] Nummer; Zahl; Ziffer; **number plate** [ˈnʌmbəpleɪt] Nummernschild

o'clock [əˈklɒk]: **10 o'clock** 10 Uhr
October [ɒkˈtəʊbə] Oktober
of [ɒv, əv] von; **a bottle of milk** eine Flasche Milch; **the name of the sport** der Name der Sportart
often [ˈɒfn] oft
OK [əʊˈkeɪ] okay, (schon) gut, in Ordnung
old [əʊld] alt
on [ɒn] 1. auf; 2. an, eingeschaltet; **on Monday** am Montag; montags **on Sundays** sonntags; **on TV** im Fernsehen
one [wʌn] ein/eine; eine/einer/eines
only [ˈəʊnli] nur, bloß; erst
open [ˈəʊpən] 1. öffnen, aufmachen; aufschlagen; 2. offen, geöffnet; **open day** Tag der offenen Tür
opposite [ˈɒpəzɪt] Gegenteil
or [ɔː] oder
orange [ˈɒrɪndʒ] Orange, Apfelsine

other [ˈʌðə] andere, weitere
our [ˈaʊə] unser/unsere
over there [əʊvəˈðeə] da drüben, dort drüben

P

page [peɪdʒ] Seite
paint [peɪnt] malen; (an)streichen
Pakistan [pɑːkɪˈstɑːn] Pakistan
parent, parents [ˈpeərənt, ˈpeərənts] Elternteil, Eltern
park [pɑːk] parken; **car park** Parkhaus, *(großer)* Parkplatz; **fun park** Freizeitpark, Erlebnispark, Vergnügungspark
partner [ˈpɑːtnə] Partner/Partnerin
pen [pen] Füller
pence (p) [pens, piː] Pence *(brit. Geld)*
pencil [ˈpensl] Bleistift
pencil-case [ˈpenslkeɪs] Federmäppchen, Schreibetui
people [ˈpiːpl] Leute, Menschen
perhaps [pəˈhæps] vielleicht
pet shop [ˈpetʃɒp] Kleintierhandlung, Zoohandlung
phone [fəʊn] Telefon
photo [ˈfəʊtəʊ] Foto; **in my photo** auf meinem Foto; **take photos** Fotos machen, fotografieren
picture [ˈpɪktʃə] Bild, Foto
pig [pɪg] Schwein
pink [pɪŋk] rosa, pink
place [pleɪs] Ort, Platz, Stelle
plan [plæn] planen, vorhaben
plant [plɑːnt] Pflanze
plate [pleɪt]: **number plate** Nummernschild
play [pleɪ] spielen; **play sport** Sport treiben
please [pliːz] bitte
plural [ˈplʊərəl] Plural, Mehrzahl
pocket-money [ˈpɒkɪtˈmʌni] Taschengeld
pop [pɒp] Pop(musik)
popular [ˈpɒpjələ] beliebt
postcard [ˈpəʊstkɑːd] Postkarte, Ansichtskarte
poster [ˈpəʊstə] Poster
potato, potatoes [pəˈteɪtəʊ, pəˈteɪtəʊz] Kartoffel, Kartoffeln
pound (£) [paʊnd] Pfund *(brit. Geld)*
price [praɪs] (Kauf-)Preis
programme [ˈprəʊgræm] (Radio-, Fernseh-)Sendung
pullover [ˈpʊləʊvə] Pullover

pupil [ˈpjuːpl] Schüler/Schülerin
put [pʊt] stellen; legen; *(an einen Platz)* tun; **Put your hands up.** Hebt die Hände hoch.

Q

question [ˈkwestʃən] Frage
quiz [kwɪz] Quiz

R

radio [ˈreɪdiəʊ] Radio
read [riːd] lesen, vorlesen
red [red] rot
restaurant [ˈrestərɒnt] Restaurant
ride [raɪd]: **ride a bike** (mit dem) Rad fahren; **ride on the tractor** auf dem Traktor mitfahren
right [raɪt] richtig; **You're right.** Du hast Recht.
road [rəʊd] Straße
roll [rəʊl] Brötchen
room [ruːm] Zimmer, Raum
rubber [ˈrʌbə] Radiergummi
ruler [ˈruːlə] Lineal
run [rʌn] rennen, laufen

S

sad [sæd] traurig
said [sed] sagte/sagten
sandwich [ˈsænwɪtʃ] Sandwich *(belegtes Brot)*
Saturday [ˈsætədeɪ, ˈsætədi] Samstag, Sonnabend
sauce [sɔːs] Soße
say [seɪ] sagen; **O'Grady says** O'Grady sagt
school [skuːl] Schule; **at school** in der Schule; **go to school** zur Schule gehen
seaside [ˈsiːsaɪd] Küste
season [ˈsiːzn] Jahreszeit
second-hand [ˈsekəndˈhænd] aus zweiter Hand, gebraucht
see [siː]: **See you.** Bis dann.
sell [sel] verkaufen
September [sepˈtembə] September
she [ʃiː] sie
sheep [ʃiːp] Schaf, Schafe
shirt [ʃɜːt] Hemd
shop [ʃɒp] Laden, Geschäft; **go to the shops** einkaufen gehen

show [ʃəʊ] Show
sign [saɪn] Schild; Zeichen
sister [ˈsɪstə] Schwester
sit down [sɪtˈdaʊn] sich (hin)setzen
size [saɪz] Größe
skateboarding [ˈskeɪtbɔːdɪŋ] Skateboardfahren
skating [ˈskeɪtɪŋ] Schlittschuh-, Rollschuhlaufen
small [smɔːl] klein
snack [snæk] Snack, Imbiss; **snack bar** [ˈsnækbɑː] Snackbar, Imbissstube
some [sʌm] einige, ein paar
sometimes [ˈsʌmtaɪmz] manchmal
son [sʌn] Sohn
song [sɒŋ] Lied
sorry [ˈsɒri]: **I'm sorry. / Sorry.** Tut mir Leid.
spaghetti [spəˈgeti] Spaghetti
special [ˈspeʃl] besondere/besonderer/besonderes
sponge [spʌndʒ] Schwamm
sport [spɔːt] Sport, Sportart; **play sport** Sport treiben; **sports centre** Sportzentrum; **sports matches** Sportveranstaltungen
spring [sprɪŋ] Frühling
stall [stɔːl] (Verkaufs-)Stand
stand [stænd] stehen; **stand up** [stændˈʌp] aufstehen
start [stɑːt]: **Start here.** Fang/Fangt hier an.
stay [steɪ] bleiben
story [ˈstɔːri] Geschichte, Erzählung
stupid [ˈstjuːpɪd] dumm, blöd
summer [ˈsʌmə] Sommer
Sunday [ˈsʌndeɪ, ˈsʌndi] Sonntag
super [ˈsuːpə] super, toll
supermarket [ˈsuːpəmɑːkɪt] Supermarkt
sure [ʃʊə] sicher
surprise [səˈpraɪz] Überraschung; Überraschungs-
sweatshirt [ˈswetʃɜːt] Sweatshirt
sweet [swiːt] Süßigkeit, Bonbon
swim [swɪm] schwimmen

T

T-shirt [ˈtiːʃɜːt] T-Shirt
table [ˈteɪbl] Tisch
take [teɪk]: **take-away ...** [teɪkəˈweɪ] ... zum Mitnehmen; **take photos** Fotos machen, fotografieren

taxi ['tæksi] Taxi
teacher ['tiːtʃə] Lehrer/Lehrerin
team [tiːm] Team, Mannschaft
teeth [tiːθ]: **I clean my teeth.**
Ich putze mir die Zähne.
telephone ['telɪfəʊn] Telefon
tennis ['tenɪs] Tennis
terrible ['terəbl] schrecklich, fürchterlich
than [ðæn]: **nicer than** schöner als,
besser als
thank [θæŋk]: **Thank you.** Danke
(schön). **Thanks.** [θæŋks] Danke.
Thanksgiving Day [θæŋks'gɪvɪŋdeɪ]
Erntedankfest
that [ðæt] das; der/die/das (da)
the [ðə, ði] der/die/das
their [ðeə] ihr/ihre
them [ðem, ðəm] ihnen/sie
then [ðen] dann
there [ðeə] da, dort; dahin, dorthin;
there are da sind, es gibt, es sind;
there's (= there is) da ist, es gibt,
es ist
they [ðeɪ] sie
thing [θɪŋ] Ding, Sache
thirsty ['θɜːsti] durstig; **I'm thirsty.**
Ich habe Durst.
this [ðɪs] dies/das (hier); diese/dieser/
dieses
throw [θrəʊ]: **throw (at)** werfen
(nach)
Thursday ['θɜːzdeɪ, 'θɜːzdi] Donnerstag
till [tɪl] bis
time [taɪm] Zeit; Uhrzeit; **What time
is it?** Wie spät ist es?
tip [tɪp] Tipp, Hinweis
to [tuː, tu, tə] zu, nach; an
today [tə'deɪ] heute
toilet ['tɔɪlət] Toilette
tomorrow [tə'mɒrəʊ] morgen
too [tuː] **1.** auch; **2. too late** zu spät
tool [tuːl] Werkzeug
town [taʊn] Stadt; **go to town**
in die Stadt gehen; **in town**
in der (Innen-) Stadt
toy [tɔɪ] Spielzeug; **toy-shop** Spielzeuggeschäft
tractor ['træktə] Traktor
train [treɪn] Zug, Eisenbahn
Tuesday ['tjuːzdeɪ, 'tjuːzdi] Dienstag
TV ['tiː'viː] Fernsehen; Fernsehgerät;
TV programme Fernsehsendung;
on TV im Fernsehen; **watch TV**
fernsehen

U

uncle ['ʌŋkl] Onkel
unfriendly [ʌn'frendli] unfreundlich
us [ʌs] uns

V

very ['veri] sehr
video ['vɪdiəʊ] Videofilm, Video;
video recorder ['vɪdiəʊrɪ'kɔːdə]
Videorecorder
village ['vɪlɪdʒ] Dorf
visit ['vɪzɪt] besuchen; besichtigen

W

walk [wɔːk] (zu Fuß) gehen, laufen;
wandern
walkman ['wɔːkmən] Walkman
wallet ['wɒlɪt] Brieftasche
wallpaper ['wɔːlpeɪpə] Tapete
want [wɒnt] wollen; **want to go**
gehen wollen
was [wɒz, wəz] war
wash [wɒʃ]: **have a wash** sich
waschen; **wash up** [wɒʃ'ʌp]
abwaschen, spülen
watch [wɒtʃ] zusehen, sich anschauen, beobachten; **watch TV**
fernsehen
we [wiː] wir
Wednesday ['wenzdeɪ, 'wenzdi]
Mittwoch
week [wiːk] Woche
weekday ['wiːkdeɪ] Wochentag
weekend [wiːk'end] Wochenende;
at the weekend am Wochenende
well [wel]: **Well, ...** Nun, ...
wet [wet] nass, feucht
what [wɒt] **1.** was; **2.** welche/wel-
cher/welches; **What about ...?**
Wie wäre es mit ...? Was ist mit ...?;
What colour is ...? Welche Farbe
hat ...? **What time is it?** Wie spät
ist es? **What's ... in English?** Wie
heißt ... auf Englisch? **What's the
matter?** Was ist los? **What's your
name?** Wie heißt du? / Wie heißen
Sie?
when [wen] wann
where [weə] wo; wohin; **Where are
you from?** Wo kommst du her?
white [waɪt] weiß

who [huː] wer
why [waɪ] warum, weshalb
wife [waɪf] Ehefrau
will [wɪl]: **I will go** ich werde gehen
window ['wɪndəʊ] Fenster, Schaufenster
winter ['wɪntə] Winter
with [wɪð] mit; bei
woman, women ['wʊmən, 'wɪmɪn]
Frau, Frauen
won't [wəʊnt] **(= will not): I won't go**
ich werde nicht gehen
word [wɜːd] Wort
work [wɜːk] arbeiten; funktionieren
would [wʊd]: **What would you like?**
Was hätten Sie gern? **I'd like**
[aɪd'laɪk] **(= I would like) ...** Ich
möchte ... / Ich hätte gern ...
write [raɪt] schreiben
wrong [rɒŋ] falsch

Y

year [jɪə] Jahr; Jahrgang
yellow ['jeləʊ] gelb
yes [jes] ja
yoghurt ['jɒgət] Joghurt
you [juː] **1.** du; ihr; Sie; **2.** man
young [jʌŋ] jung
your [jɔː] dein/deine; euer/eure;
Ihr/Ihre

Z

zoo [zuː] Zoo

Wörterverzeichnis

Alphabetische Liste der Wörter aus Band 1 (Deutsch – Englisch)

A

Abend evening; *(später Abend)* night;
  Guten Abend. Good evening.
abends in the evening(s)
aber but
abfahren leave
abwaschen wash up
Abzeichen badge
Ahnung idea
Alarm; Alarmanlage alarm
alle all; all the
alles 1. all; **2.** everything
als: schöner als nicer than
alt old
am: am billigsten the cheapest;
  am Abend/Morgen/Nachmittag
  in the evening(s)/morning(s)/after-
  noon(s); **am Montag** on Monday;
  am Wochenende at the weekend
Amerikaner/in; amerikanisch American
an 1. at; **2.** to; **3.** *(eingeschaltet)* on
andere/r/s; anders (als) different
  (from); **andere** *(weitere)* other
anfangen: Fang/t hier an. Start here.
Anhänger/in fan
anhören: sich anhören listen to
anschauen: sich anschauen watch
ansehen, sich ansehen look at
Ansichtskarte postcard
Anstecker badge
anstreichen paint
Antwort (auf) answer (to)
Apfel apple
Apfelsine orange
April April
Arbeit job
arbeiten work
auch too
auf on; **auf dem Land** in the country;
  auf Englisch in English;
  auf meinem Foto in my photo;
  Auf Wiedersehen. Goodbye.
Aufgabe job
aufmachen; aufschlagen open
aufstehen 1. stand up; **2.** *(aus dem
  Bett)* get up
Augenblick: Einen Augenblick.
  Just a minute.
August August

aus *(„aus England")* from
Auto car

B

Bad, Badezimmer bathroom
Ball ball
Banane banana
Batterie battery
Bauernhof farm; **Spielzeugbauernhof** farm set
Baukasten building set
Bayern Bavaria
Becher *(Karton)* carton
bei 1. at; **2.** with; **bei uns/Asif
  (zu Hause)** at our house / at
  Asif's flat
belebt busy
beliebt popular
beobachten watch
Beruf job
beschäftigt busy
besichtigen visit
besondere/r/s special
besuchen visit
Bett bed; **ins Bett gehen** go to
  bed
Bild picture
billig cheap
bin: ich bin I'm (= I am)
bis till; **Bis dann.** See you.
bist: du bist you're (= you are)
bitte please; **Hier, bitte.** Here
  you are.
blau blue
bleiben stay
Bleistift pencil
blöd stupid
bloß only
Bonbon sweet
brauchen need
braun brown
brechen break
Brief letter
Brieftasche wallet
bringen bring
Brötchen roll
Bruder brother
Buch book
Bücherei library

Bus bus
Button badge

C

Café café
Cassette cassette
CD CD
Cent cent
Cheeseburger cheeseburger
Cola cola
Comic(heft) comic
Computer computer
Cousin/Cousine cousin

D

da there; **da ist** there's; **da sind**
  there are; **da drüben** over there
daheim at home
dahin there
Danke. Thanks. *(Danke schön.)*
  Thank you.
dann then; **Bis dann.** See you.
das the; *(das da)* that; *(das hier)* this;
  Das ist toll. That's great.
dein/e your
der the; *(der da)* that
deutsch; Deutsch; Deutsche/r German
Deutschland Germany
Dezember December
Dialog dialogue
dich you
die the; **die (da)** *(Einzahl)* that
Dienstag Tuesday
dies (hier) this
diese/r/s this
Ding thing
dir you
Donnerstag Thursday
Dorf village
dort; dorthin there; **dort drüben**
  over there
Drachen *(Papierdrachen)* kite
du you
dumm stupid
dürfen c/an; **ich darf nicht** I can't
Durst: Ich habe Durst. I'm thirsty.
durstig thirsty

137

E

Egal. Never mind.
Ehefrau wife
ein/e 1. a ("town"), an ("exercise");
  2. one
eine/r/s one
Einfall idea
eingeschaltet on
einige some
einkaufen gehen go to the shops
einsammeln collect
Eis (Speiseeis) ice-cream
Eisenbahn train
Eltern, Elternteil parents, parent
England England
Engländer/in: ich bin Engländer/in
  I'm English
englisch; Englisch English;
  auf Englisch in English
Entschuldigen Sie, … Excuse me, …
er 1. he; **2.** it (nicht bei Personen)
Erlebnispark fun park
Erntedankfest Thanksgiving Day
erst only
erste/r/s first
Erzählung story
es it; **es ist/gibt** there's; **es sind/**
  gibt there are
essen eat
Essen food; (zubereitet) meal
Etui (Schreibetui) pencil-case
etwas: Sonst noch etwas?
  Anything else?
euch you
euer/eure your
Euro euro
Europa Europe

F

fahren go; **(mit dem) Rad fahren** ri-
  de a bike
Fahrrad bike
falsch wrong; **falscher Alarm**
  false alarm
Familie family
Fan fan
Farbe colour; **Welche Farbe hat …?**
  What colour is …?
Farm farm
Februar February
Federmäppchen pencil-case
Feiertag holiday
Feld field

Fenster window
Ferien holiday
fernsehen watch TV
Fernsehen; Fernsehgerät TV;
  im Fernsehen on TV
Fernsehsendung TV programme
feucht wet
Film film
Filzstift felt-tip
finden find
Fisch, Fische fish; **Fisch und Pom-**
  mes frites fish and chips
Flasche bottle; **eine Flasche Milch**
  a bottle of milk
Foto photo, picture; **Fotos machen**
  take photos; **auf meinem Foto**
  in my photo
Fotoapparat camera
fotografieren take photos
Frage question
Frau, Frauen woman, women;
  (vor Namen) Mrs
frei free
Freitag Friday
Freizeit free time
Freizeitpark fun park
fressen: zu fressen geben feed
Freund/in friend; **(feste) Freundin**
  girlfriend
freundlich friendly
Frikadelle burger
Frühling spring
Frühstück breakfast
frühstücken have breakfast
Füller pen
funktionieren work
für for
fürchterlich terrible
Fußball football
Futter food
füttern feed

G

Garage garage
Gardine curtain
Garten garden
geben: es gibt 1. (Einzahl) there's
  (= there is); **2.** (Mehrzahl) there are;
  zu fressen geben feed
gebraucht second-hand
gebrochen broken
Gegenteil opposite
gehen go; (zu Fuß gehen) walk; **ein-**
  kaufen gehen go to the shops

gelangweilt bored
gelb yellow
Geld money
genug enough
geöffnet open
gern: gern haben like; **Ich fahre**
  gern Skateboard. I like skate-
  boarding. **Ich hätte gern …**
  I'd like …; **Was hätten Sie gern?**
  What would you like?
Geschäft shop
Geschichte story
geschickt in good at
Gespräch dialogue
Getränk drink
Getreide cereal
Glück: du hast Glück you're lucky
glücklich: glücklicher Asif lucky Asif
Größe size
groß big
großartig great
Großbritannien Britain
Großmutter grandma, grandmother
Großvater grandfather
grün green
Gruppe group
Gummibärchen jelly baby
gut 1. good; **2.** (in Ordnung) OK;
  gut in good at; **Guten Abend.**
  Good evening. **Guten Morgen.**
  Good morning. **Guten Tag.** Good
  afternoon. (nachmittags) / Hallo.

H

haben have
Hähnchen (Brathähnchen) chicken
Hallo. Hallo. / Hi.
Hamburger hamburger, burger
Hand: aus zweiter Hand second-
  hand; **Hebt die Hände hoch.**
  Put your hands up.
Handlung action
hatte/n had
hätte: Ich hätte gern … I'd like …;
  Was hätten Sie gern? What would
  you like?
Haus house; **nach Hause** home;
  zu Hause at home; **bei uns/Asif zu**
  Hause at our house / at Asif's flat
Heft book
heim; Heim home
heißen: Was heißt … auf Englisch?
  What's … in English? **Wie heißt du /**
  heißen Sie? What's your name?

hektisch busy
helfen help
Hemd shirt
Herbst autumn
Herr *(vor Namen)* Mr
herstellen make
heute today
hier; hierhin/-her here; **Hier, bitte.**
  Here you are.
hinsetzen: sich hinsetzen sit down
Hinweis tip
Hobby hobby
hochheben: Hebt die Hände hoch.
  Put your hands up.
Hockey hockey
hören, sich anhören listen to
Hot Dog hot dog
Huhn chicken
Hund dog
Hunger: Ich habe Hunger. I'm hungry.
hungrig hungry

ich I
Idee idea
ihm; ihn 1. him; **2.** it *(nicht bei Personen)*
ihnen them
ihr 1. *("ihr seid")* you; **2.** *("mit ihr")* it *(nicht bei Personen)*
ihr/e 1. *(Einzahl)* **a.** her; **b.** its *(nicht bei Personen)*; **2.** *(Mehrzahl)* their
Ihr/e your
im: im Fernsehen on TV; **im Januar** in January
Imbiss snack
Imbissstube snack bar
immer always
in 1. in; **2.** at; **in der Nähe von** near; **in der (Innen-)Stadt** in town; **in der Schule** at school; **in die Stadt gehen** go to town; **ins Bett gehen** go to bed
interessant interesting
ist is (he's/she's/it's)

ja yes
Jahr year
Jahreszeit season
Jahrgang year
Januar January

Jeans jeans
jede/r/s every
jetzt now
Joghurt yoghurt
Juli July
jung young
Junge boy
Juni June

Kabelfernsehen cable TV
Kamera camera
kaputt broken
kaputtmachen break
Kartoffel, Kartoffeln potato, potatoes
Kartoffelchips crisps
Karton carton
Käse cheese
Katze cat
kaufen buy
Kaufpreis price
kein/e no
kennen lernen meet
Ketchup ketchup
Kind, Kinder child, children
Kino cinema
Kissen cushion
Klasse class
Klassenzimmer classroom
Kleider, Kleidung clothes
klein small
Kleinbus minibus
Kleintierhandlung pet shop
Kochen cooking
Kofferraum car-boot
kommen come; **Komm schon!** Come on! **Wir werden zu spät kommen.** We'll be late. **Wo kommst du her?** Where are you from?
können can; **ich kann nicht** I can't **Kann ich bitte ... haben?** Can I have ..., please? **Können wir ein/e ... haben?** Can we have a ...?
kosten cost; **Was kostet/kosten ...?** How much is/are ...?
kostenlos free
krank ill
Kreditkarte credit card
Küche kitchen
Kuchen cake
Kugelschreiber biro
Kuh cow
Kunde/Kundin customer
Küste seaside

lachen laugh
Laden shop
Land country; **auf dem Land** in the country
lang long
langweilen: ich langweile mich I'm bored
lassen *(liegen/stehen lassen)* leave; **Lasst uns gehen!** Let's go!
laufen walk; *(schnell)* run
leben live
Lebensmittel food
leer empty
legen put
Lehrer/in teacher
Leid: Tut mir Leid. (I'm) Sorry.
lesen read
Leute people
Lieblings- favourite
Lied song
liegen lassen leave
Limonade lemonade
Lineal ruler
los: Los! Come on! **Was ist los?** What's the matter?

machen do; make; **... macht/ machen Spaß.** ... is/are fun. **Fotos machen** take photos; **Macht nichts.** Never mind.
Mädchen girl
März March
Mahlzeit meal
Mai May
malen paint
Mama mum
man you
manchmal sometimes
Mann, Männer man, men
Mannschaft team
Markt market
Markthalle market hall
Mathe(matik) maths
Mehrzahl plural
mein/e my
Menschen people
mich me
Milch milk
Milchmixgetränk milk shake
Minute minute
mir me

mit with; **Was ist mit …? Wie wäre es mit …?** What about …?
mitbringen bring
mitfahren: auf dem Traktor mitfahren ride on the tractor
Mitte centre
Mittwoch Wednesday
Modell model
modern modern
mögen like; **Ich möchte …** I'd like …
Monat month
Montag Monday
montags on Monday
morgen tomorrow
Morgen morning; **Guten Morgen.** Good morning.
morgens in the morning(s)
Mountainbike mountain bike
Museum museum
Musik music
Mutter mother
Mutti mum

nach 1. (*„nach drei Monaten"*) after; **2.** *(zu)* to; **nach Hause** home
Nachbar/in neighbour
Nachbildung model
Nachmittag afternoon
nachmittags in the afternoon(s)
Nacht night
nächste/r/s next
nah; in der Nähe von near
Name name
nass wet
neben next to
nein no
nett nice
neu new
Neujahrstag New Year's Day
nicht not
nichts: Macht nichts. Never mind.
nie(mals) never
noch: noch einmal again; **Sonst noch etwas?** Anything else?
November November
Nummer number
Nummernschild number plate
nun now; **Nun, …** Well, …
nur only

oder or
offen open; **Tag der offenen Tür** open day
öffnen open
oft often
okay OK
Oktober October
Oma grandma
Onkel uncle
Orange orange
Ordnung: in Ordnung OK
Ort place

paar: ein paar some
Pakistan Pakistan
Papa dad
parken park
Parkhaus, (großer) Parkplatz car park
Partner/in partner
Party party
Pence pence (p)
Pflanze plant
Pfund *(britisches Geld)* pound (£)
planen plan
Platz place
Plural plural
Pommes frites chips
Pommes-frites-Bude chip shop
Pop(musik) pop
Poster poster
Postkarte postcard
Preis *(Kaufpreis)* price
preiswert cheap
pro: 3 Pfund pro Woche £3 a week
Pullover pullover
Puppe doll
putzen: Ich putze mir die Zähne. I clean my teeth.

Q

Quiz quiz

R

Rad *(Fahrrad)* bike; **(mit dem) Rad fahren** ride a bike
Radiergummi rubber

Radio radio
Raum room
Rechner computer
Recht: Du hast Recht. You're right.
rennen run
Restaurant restaurant
richtig right
Rollschuhlaufen skating
rosa pink
rot red

S

Sache thing
Saft juice
sagen say; **sagt: O'Grady sagt** O'Grady says; **sagte/n** said
sammeln collect
Samstag Saturday
Sandwich sandwich
Schaf, Schafe sheep
schauen look
Schaufenster window
Schild sign
Schlafzimmer bedroom
Schlittschuhlaufen skating
Schokolade chocolate
schon gut OK
schön nice
Schrank cupboard
schrecklich terrible
schreiben write
Schreibetui pencil-case
Schule school; **in der Schule** at school; **zur Schule gehen** go to school
Schüler/in pupil
Schultasche bag
Schwamm sponge
schwarz black
Schwein pig
Schwester sister
schwimmen swim
sehen look
sehr very
seid: ihr seid you're (= you are)
sein be
sein/e 1. his; **2.** its *(nicht bei Personen)*
Seite page
Sendung *(Radio-, Fernsehsendung)* progamme
September September
setzen: sich (hin)setzen sit down
Show show

sicher sure
sie *(Einzahl)* **1.** she; **2.** it *(nicht bei Personen)*; **3.** *(„für sie")* it *(nicht bei Personen)*
sie *(Mehrzahl)* **1.** they; **2.** *(„für sie")* them
Sie you
sind are (we're/you're/they're)
Skateboardfahren skateboarding
Snack snack
Snackbar snack bar
Sohn son
Sommer summer
Sonnabend Saturday
Sonntag Sunday
sonntags on Sundays
Sonst noch etwas? Anything else?
sorgfältig careful
Soße sauce
Spaghetti spaghetti
Spaß fun; **... macht/machen Spaß.** ... is/are fun.
spät late; **Wir werden zu spät kommen.** We'll be late. **Wie spät ist es?** What time is it?
Speise meal
Speiseeis ice-cream
Spiel game; *(Wettkampf)* match
spielen play
Spielzeug toy
Spielzeugbauernhof farm set
Spielzeuggeschäft toy-shop
Sport, Sportart sport; **Sport treiben** play sport
Sportveranstaltungen sports matches
Sportzentrum sports centre
spülen wash up
Stadt town; **in der (Innen-)Stadt** in town; **in die Stadt gehen** go to town
Stand *(Verkaufsstand)* stall
stehen stand; **stehen lassen** leave
Stelle place
stellen put
Straße road
streichen paint
Stuhl chair
Stunde *(Unterrichtsstunde)* lesson
super super
Supermarkt supermarket
Süßigkeit sweet
Sweatshirt sweatshirt

T-Shirt T-shirt
Tafel board
Tag day; **Tag der offenen Tür** open day; **Guten Tag.** Good afternoon. *(nachmittags)* / Hallo.
Tante aunt
Tapete wallpaper
Tasche bag
Taschengeld pocket-money
Taschenrechner calculator
Tätigkeit action
Taxi taxi
Team team
Telefon (tele)phone
Tennis tennis
teuer expensive
Tier animal; **Kleintierhandlung** pet shop
Tierheim animal home
Tipp tip
Tisch table
Tochter daughter
Toilette toilet
toll great, super
Traktor tractor; **auf dem Traktor mitfahren** ride on the tractor
traurig sad
treffen, sich treffen (mit) meet
treiben: Sport treiben play sport
Trinkschokolade chocolate
Trödelmarkt car-boot sale
Tschüs. Bye. / Bye-bye.
tun do; *(an einen Platz tun)* put; **Tut mir Leid.** (I'm) Sorry.
Tür door
Tüte bag

über 1. *(„über dem Geschäft")* above; **2.** *(„über etwas reden")* about
Überraschung; Überraschungs- surprise
Übung exercise
Uhr clock; **10 Uhr** 10 o'clock
Uhrzeit time
um 10 Uhr at 10 o'clock
Unabhängigkeitstag Independence Day
und and
unfreundlich unfriendly
uns us
unser/e our

Unterrichtsstunde lesson
Urlaub holiday

V

Vater father
Vati dad
Vergnügungspark fun park
verkaufen sell
Verkaufsstand stall
verlassen leave
verschieden different
verspätet late
Vetter cousin
Video(film) video
Videorecorder video recorder
viel; viele lots of
vielleicht perhaps
voll: voller Autos full of cars
von 1. from; **2.** of; **von 8 (Uhr) bis 10 (Uhr)** from 8 till 10
vor *(„vor dem Haus")* in front of
vorhaben plan
Vorhang curtain
vorlesen read
Vormittag morning
vormittags in the mornings(s)
vorsichtig careful

W

Walkman walkman
wandern walk
wann when
war was
warum why
was what; **Was für ein/e ...!** What a ...! **Was heißt ... auf Englisch?** What's ... in English? **Was ist los?** What's the matter? **Was ist mit ...?** What about ...? **Was kostet/ kosten ...?** How much is/are ...?
waschen: sich waschen have a wash
weggehen von leave
Weihnachten Christmas
Weihnachtstag: der erste Weihnachtstag Christmas Day
weiß white
weit far
weitere other
welche/r/s what; **Welche Farbe hat ...?** What colour is ...?
wer who

werden: **ich werde gehen** I'll (= I
will) go; **ich werde nicht gehen**
I won't go
werfen (nach) throw (at)
Werkzeug tool
weshalb why
Wettkampf match
wie how; **Wie alt bist du?** How old
are you? **Wie heißt du / heißen
Sie?** What's your name? **Wie spät
ist es?** What time is it? **Wie wäre
es mit ...?** What about ...?
wieder again
Wiedersehen. Bye. / Bye-bye.
Auf Wiedersehen. Goodbye.
Wiese field
Winter winter
wir we
wo where; **Wo kommst du her?**
Where are you from?

Woche week
Wochenende weekend; **am
Wochenende** at the weekend
Wochentag weekday
wohin where
wohnen live
Wohnung flat
Wohnzimmer living-room
wollen want; **gehen wollen**
want to go
Wort word

Z

Zahl number
zählen count
Zähne: Ich putze mir die Zähne.
I clean my teeth.
Zeichen sign

Zeit time
Zeitschrift magazine
Zentrum centre
zerbrechen break
zerbrochen broken
Ziffer number
Zimmer room
Zoo zoo
Zoohandlung pet shop
zu 1. *(nach)* to; **2.** *(„zu spät")*
too;
zu Hause at home; **... zum
Mitnehmen** take-away ...;
zur Schule gehen go to school
Zuhause home
Zug train
zuhören listen
zusehen watch
zweite Hand: aus zweiter Hand
second-hand

LIST OF NAMES

■ GIRLS/WOMEN

Alison	['ælɪsn]
Ann	[æn]
Aysha	['eɪʃə]
Bina	['biːnə]
Claire	[kleə]
Emma	['emə]
Hannah	['hænə]
Jean	[dʒiːn]
Jenny	['dʒeni]
Jill	[dʒɪl]
Julia	['dʒuːliə]
Karen	['kærən]
Kate	[keɪt]
Liz	[lɪz]
Lucy	['luːsi]

Sally	['sæli]
Sarah	['seərə]
Sharon	['ʃærən]
Sue	[suː]
Susan	['suːzn]
Tina	['tiːnə]

■ BOYS/MEN

Adam	['ædəm]
Al	[æl]
Alan	['ælən]
Asif	['æsiːf]
Bill	[bɪl]
Ben	[ben]
Dan	[dæn]
Dave	[deɪv]
Dennis	['denɪs]
Derek	['derɪk]

Eric	['erɪk]
Grant	[grɑːnt]
Hanif	['hæniːf]
Joe	[dʒəʊ]
Kevin	['kevɪn]
Luke	[luːk]
Mark	[mɑːk]
Martin	['mɑːtɪn]
Mike	[maɪk]
Nick	[nɪk]
Pete	[piːt]
Peter	['piːtə]
Sam	[sæm]
Simon	['saɪmən]
Tariq	['tærɪk]
Tom	[tɒm]

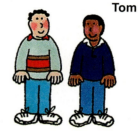

■ FAMILIES

Ahmed	[ˈɑːmed]
Ambrose	[ˈæmbrəʊz]
Baker	[ˈbeɪkə]
Bakewell	[ˈbeɪkwel]
Bedford	[ˈbedfəd]
Brown	[braʊn]
Burton	[ˈbɜːtn]
Dale	[deɪl]
Dean	[diːn]
Fry	[fraɪ]
Glenn	[glen]
Green	[griːn]
Hall	[hɔːl]
Hill	[hɪl]
Johnson	[ˈdʒɒnsn]
Kelly	[ˈkeli]
Khan	[kɑːn]
Lee	[liː]
Low	[ləʊ]
Parks	[pɑːks]
Payne	[peɪn]
Reed	[riːd]
Richardson	[ˈrɪtʃədsn]
Smith	[smɪθ]
Steel	[stiːl]
Tate	[teɪt]

■ PLACES

Brookland School	[ˈbrʊklənd ˈskuːl]
Chester	[ˈtʃestə]
Elm Road	[ˈelm ˈrəʊd]
King School	[ˈkɪŋ ˈskuːl]
London	[ˈlʌndən]
London Road	[ˈlʌndən ˈrəʊd]
Rosedale Farm	[ˈrəʊzdeɪl ˈfɑːm]
Stockwell	[ˈstɒkwel]
Woodlake	[ˈwʊdleɪk]
York	[jɔːk]

■ OTHER NAMES

Australian Friends	[ɒˈstreɪliən ˈfrendz]
Beano	[ˈbiːnəʊ]
Billy Whizz	[ˈbɪlɪ ˈwɪz]
Boris	[ˈbɒrɪs]
Brown Cow	[ˈbraʊn ˈkaʊ]
Bunty	[ˈbʌnti]
Burger World	[ˈbɜːgə ˈwɜːld]
Buster	[ˈbʌstə]
Chox	[tʃɒks]
Cortino	[kɔːˈtiːnəʊ]
Dandy	[ˈdændi]
Dinky doll	[ˈdɪŋki ˈdɒl]
Fry's TV Service	[ˈfraɪztiːˈviːˈsɜːvɪs]
Guy Fawkes	[ˈgaɪ ˈfɔːks]
Halloween	[ˈhæləʊˈiːn]
Hickory, dickory, dock	[ˈhɪkəri ˈdɪkəri ˈdɒk]
Jacko	[ˈdʒækəʊ]
Kids	[kɪdz]
Laura Lee TV Show	[ˈlɔːrə ˈliːtiːˈviːˈʃəʊ]
Longer Life	[ˈlɒŋgə ˈlaɪf]
Manchester City	[ˈmæntʃɪstə ˈsiti]
Manchester United	[ˈmæntʃɪstəjuˈnaɪtɪd]
Naido	[ˈnaɪdəʊ]
O'Grady	[əʊˈgreɪdi]
Pupilmatic	[ˈpjuːplˈmætɪk]]
Sesame Street	[ˈsesəmistriːt]
Sky	[skaɪ]
Speed bike	[ˈspiːdbaɪk]
Sports Time	[ˈspɔːtstaɪm]]
Sprint	[sprɪnt]
Star	[stɑː]
Superdog	[ˈsuːpədɒg]
TeenScene	[ˈtiːnsiːn]
Terry	[ˈteri]
The Music Show	[ðəˈmjuːzɪkʃəʊ]
Topper	[ˈtɒpə]
Vid Kid	[ˈvɪdkɪd]

THE ENGLISH ALPHABET

a	[eɪ]
b	[biː]
c	[siː]
d	[diː]
e	[iː]
f	[ef]
g	[dʒiː]
h	[eɪtʃ]
i	[aɪ]
j	[dʒeɪ]
k	[keɪ]
l	[el]
m	[em]
n	[en]
o	[əʊ]
p	[piː]
q	[kjuː]
r	[aː]
s	[es]
t	[tiː]
u	[juː]
v	[viː]
w	['dʌbljuː]
x	[eks]
y	[waɪ]
z	[zed]

ENGLISH SOUNDS

[iː]	meet, team, he
[aː]	answer, class, car
[ɔː]	or, ball, door
[uː]	ruler, blue, too
[ɜː]	girl, word, her
[i]	radio, video, sorry
[u]	July, February
[ɪ]	in, enough, big
[e]	empty, yes, bed
[æ]	cat, black
[ʌ]	bus, come
[ɒ]	on, dog, what
[ʊ]	put, good, woman
[ə]	again, today, sister
[eɪ]	eight, name, play
[aɪ]	I, time, my
[ɔɪ]	boy, toilet
[əʊ]	old, no, road
[aʊ]	house, now
[ɪə]	near, here, we're
[eə]	there, chair
[ʊə]	you're, plural
[b]	bike, hobby, job
[p]	pen, pupil, shop
[d]	day, window, good
[t]	ten, matter, at
[k]	car, lucky, book
[g]	go, again, bag
[ŋ]	wrong, morning
[l]	like, old, small
[r]	ruler, friend, biro
[v]	very, seven, have
[w]	we, swim
[s]	six, poster, yes
[z]	zoo, visit, his
[ʃ]	she, action, English
[tʃ]	child, teacher, match
[dʒ]	jeans, German, badge
[j]	yes, you, young
[θ]	thing, maths, month
[ð]	the, father, with

ENGLISH NUMBERS

1	one	[wʌn]
2	two	[tuː]
3	three	[θriː]
4	four	[fɔː]
5	five	[faɪv]
6	six	[sɪks]
7	seven	['sevn]
8	eight	[eɪt]
9	nine	[naɪn]
10	ten	[ten]
11	eleven	[ɪ'levn]
12	twelve	[twelv]
13	thirteen	['θɜː'tiːn]
14	fourteen	['fɔː'tiːn]
15	fifteen	['fɪf'tiːn]
16	sixteen	['sɪks'tiːn]
17	seventeen	['sevn'tiːn]
18	eighteen	['eɪ'tiːn]
19	nineteen	['naɪn'tiːn]
20	twenty	['twenti]
21	twenty-one	['twenti'wʌn]
30	thirty	['θɜːti]
40	forty	['fɔːti]
50	fifty	['fɪfti]
60	sixty	['sɪksti]
70	seventy	['sevnti]
80	eighty	['eɪti]
90	ninety	['naɪnti]
100	a hundred	[ə'hʌndrəd]

Bildquellen

Inhalt Susan Abbey, Berlin (S. 34 Bild 8);
Anna Baker, York (S. 10; S. 16 Bild 2; S. 24 oben;
S. 44 oben links; S. 72 oben links; S. 86; S. 87; S. 94
Bild 5; S. 100; S. 104 unten rechts); Barnaby's Picture
Library, London (S. 94 Bild 6); BBC, London (S. 34
Bild 3); Bildarchiv Engelmeier, Hamburg (S. 31
Bilder 2, 4, 5); Anthony Blake Photo Library,
Richmond (S. 63 Mitte / Joy Skipper); Britische
Zentrale für Fremdenverkehr, Frankfurt (S. 24 unten
links);J. Allan Cash Ltd., London (S. 94 Bild 3);
Collections, London (S. 85 rechts / Fiona Pragoff,
links / Anthea Sieveking); Deutsches Institut für
Filmkunde, Frankfurt/Main (S. 31 Bild 1);
David Dore, Guildford (S. 48 Bild 6); Angelika
Fischer, Berlin (S. 62 unten links; S. 108 unten
rechts); Fleetway Editions, London (S. 68 oben Mitte,
unten Mitte); Focus, Hamburg (S. 109 unten);
Format, London (S. 104 unten Mitte / Ulrike Preuss);
Fotex, Hamburg (S. 16 Bild 1); Hallmark Cards Inc.,
Henley-on-Thames. Reproduced with kind permis-
sion of Hallmark Cards (S. 104 Mitte links, Mitte
rechts); IFA Bilderteam, München (S. 105 /
W. Rudolph); The Image Bank, Berlin (S. 108 Mitte
rechts); Ute Klaphake, London (S. 44 oben rechts);
John Lally, York (S. 16 Bilder 3, 6, 7; S. 21; S. 24
Mitte links, Mitte Mitte; S. 34 Bilder 1, 2, 4, 5; S. 38;
S. 48 Bilder 1-5, 7; S. 52; S. 54; S. 58; S. 59 oben;
S. 60; S. 62 oben; S. 63 oben links; S. 66; S. 72
oben rechts; S. 75; S. 76 Bilder 3, 6; S. 80; S. 90
oben links, Bilder 1, 2, 4, 5, 7; S. 94 Bild 2);
Mauritius, Mittenwald (S. 34 Bild 7; S. 76 Bild 2 /
Mitterer, Bilder 4, 5 / Poehlmann); Mirror Syndication
International, London (S. 6; S. 24 Mitte rechts; S. 108
oben links, Mitte links); Musik + Show Claus Lange,
Hamburg (S. 73); NBC Europe, Unterföhring (S. 31
Bild 3); Pictor International, München (S. 104 unten
links); Henrik Pohl, Berlin (S. 8; S. 17; S. 59 Mitte,
unten links; S. 101); Paul Robson, York (S. 48 Bild 8;
S. 90 Bilder 3, 6; S. 94 Bild 4); RTL, Köln (S. 31 Bild
6); J. Salmon Ltd., Sevenoaks, Kent (S. 45 oben
rechts); Science & Society Picture Library, London
(S. 76 Bild 1 / David Exton); D.C. Thomson & Co.
Ltd., Dundee (S. 68 oben links, oben rechts, Mitte,
unten links, unten rechts); Transglobe, Hamburg
(S. 94 Bild 1); Unichrome Ltd., Bath (S. 45 oben);
Westlight International, Los Angeles (S. 104 Mitte
Mitte / Steven Chenn); H.-Joachim Zylla, Berlin
(S. 16 Bilder 4,5)
Einband Lupe Cunha, London